Overcoming Parental Anxiety

Rewire Your Brain to Worry Less & Enjoy Parenting More

Debra Kissen, PhD
Micah Ioffe, PhD
Hannah Romain, LCSW

New Harbinger Publications, Inc.

Publisher's Note

NEW HARBINGER PUBLICATIONS is a registered trademark of New Harbinger Publications, Inc.

New Harbinger Publications is an employee-owned company.

Copyright © 2022 by Debra Kissen, Micah Ioffe, Hannah Romain
New Harbinger Publications, Inc.
5674 Shattuck Avenue
Oakland, CA 94609
www.newharbinger.com

Cover design by Sara Christian; Acquired by Jennye Garibaldi; Edited by Kristi Hein

---

Library of Congress Cataloging-in-Publication Data

Names: Kissen, Debra, author. | Ioffe, Micah, author. | Romain, Hannah, author.
Title: Overcoming parental anxiety : rewire your brain to worry less and enjoy parenting more / Debra Kissen, PhD, MHSA, Micah Ioffe, PhD, Hannah Romain, LCSW.
Description: Oakland, CA : New Harbinger Publications, [2022] | Includes bibliographical references.
Identifiers: LCCN 2022026215 | ISBN 9781648480300 (trade paperback)
Subjects: LCSH: Parenting--Psychological aspects. | Parent and child--Psychological aspects. | Mindfulness (Psychology) | Cognitive therapy. | Acceptance and commitment therapy. | BISAC: FAMILY & RELATIONSHIPS / Parenting / General | PSYCHOLOGY / Neuropsychology
Classification: LCC BF723.P25 K57 2022 | DDC 155.9/24--dc23/eng/20220810
LC record available at https://lccn.loc.gov/2022026215

Printed in the United States of America

24   23   22

10   9   8   7   6   5   4   3   2   1   First Printing

Contents

Foreword

Parenting an anxious child can be a daunting task. Your child's anxiety can make them not just anxious but also demanding, irritable, and needy. Your child wants you to do something now to get rid of the anxiety fast. If you dare to research information about anxiety and kids, you likely will encounter some concerning information about how overparenting and overaccommodation makes anxiety worse. You might encounter contradictory information: one article tells you to prioritize your child's emotional attachment because failure to build a healthy attachment leads to anxiety; the next article says to ignore your child's anxious tantrum and push them to practice the thing they fear. If you are like most parents, you feel confused, pressured to get it right, and worried about your child's future. You then accidentally end up running in the same hamster wheel of worry and anxiety your child experiences. You end up feeling just as distressed as your child when you know you are supposed to be the adult who can skillfully lead them through the situation.

Overcoming Parental Anxiety is your practical and scientific guide for managing the problem that all parents of anxious children face: learning to manage their *own* anxiety while having to simultaneously teach their child how to manage their child's own anxiety. Each chapter describes key areas that challenge all parents of anxious children and provides easy-to-digest nuggets of information and effective tools that can radically improve your parenting. The authors address the problems of anxiety-reinforcing beliefs, unhelpful thought patterns, the negative effect of significant painful past experiences, and inaccurate beliefs about parenting. You'll discover a lucid explanation of how the brain's preference for attending to frightening and negative information predisposes both you and your child to choose thought patterns and behaviors that unintentionally worsen anxiety. This book also explains how practicing new thoughts and behaviors can *rewire the parent brain*, making you a more effective parent, better able to raise a more effective child. You will learn how easily your emotional reaction to your child's anxiety can either exacerbate fear or promote improved coping, based on your demeanor and words. In short, this book is your codebook to help yourself step out of self-criticism and blame for your child's anxiety and step into a calm, centered, effective parenting style that shows you know what you are doing and why.

The exercises in this book will help you become the kind of parent you admire—confident in yourself and your strategies for handling your and your child's anxiety, even when things go awry. As you set up your Training Journal and practice the exercises, you'll feel less stressed, more in control, and less burdened by the task of parenting an anxious child. You'll learn you can parent according to your highest values, no longer worrying about what other parents are doing and how your child is acting compared to others. You can let go of the parenting behaviors you feel secretly ashamed of—writing most of your teen's school paper, screaming at them because they just reneged on their promise to go to school for the forty thousandth time, or letting your ten-year-old sleep with you while your partner sleeps in the child's bed. Lastly, you will become a good role model for your child. This is especially important, because children learn much more from our actions than from our words.

This book will start you on the path to becoming not that perfect parent you wish you could be, but the parent your child needs. You are on a journey, one that shows your child how to be a human who experiences anxiety and has a good life just the same. You don't have to get it right the first time—just be willing to try, then learn from your mistakes so you can try again. This is the very example that your child most needs. I hope you enjoy the journey!

—Karen Lynn Cassiday, PhD

Author, *The No Worries Guide to Raising Your Anxious Child*; past president of the Anxiety and Depression Association of America; founder, the Anxiety Treatment Center of Greater Chicago

Introduction

If your typical day involves more moments of parenting-related stress and anxiety than joy and satisfaction, you're in good company. Parents in the United States today are actually less happy overall than childless adults, and research supports the notion that parents tend to experience more emotional pain than nonparents (Glass et al., 2016). One reason parenthood is associated with such high emotional distress is that the modern parent brain hasn't evolved much from when predators presented a real threat to helpless young children.

In humans' earlier days, a brain on parenting needed to be constantly on high alert. Life in the twenty-first century certainly presents many threats, but the kind of devoted attention and problem solving parents need to protect and care for children today is pretty different from what prehistoric parents needed. So while our species survived thanks largely to the high-alert, protective parent brain, its excessive and overactive *fight-flight-freeze* system can lead to burnout, chronic stress, and decreased life satisfaction.

As three specialized anxiety therapists, we have met with countless clients struggling to manage the emotional load that comes with the nonstop, ever-changing demands of modern parenting. While there are countless self-help books for *parents of anxious children*, we found ourselves wondering *Where are the resources for stressed-out, anxious parents?* If you are seeking relief from the stress and anxiety of being a parent, we are so glad you've found this book.

This book is your declassified guide to understanding your *parent brain*. It's filled with tips, tricks, and evidence-based exercises to decrease stress and anxiety and increase joy and vitality. As you work your way through, you will develop a better understanding of your brain on parenting. Through a range of mental fitness exercises, you'll be able to target and enhance your neurocircuitry associated with balanced, effective parenting. With a toolbox of enhanced mental capabilities, you'll be better prepared to move through and past these challenges whenever stressful parenting moments arise. You'll be able to manage these moments as a more grounded, calm, and effective parent.

You've probably already tried to decrease your stress, anxiety, or parenting challenges. So it's only natural to wonder how this book is any different from what you've already tried. We completely understand—we've worked with many parents who have felt the same way. We challenge you (and our wonderful clients) to put on your own oxygen mask first, before assisting those around you. We challenge you to view your own self-care as more than bubble baths, scented candles, or a gift card for a massage. Although moments of relaxation are wonderful and necessary, sometimes self-care is hard work! Caring for yourself means investing in yourself as a human and as a parent as you take steps to feel more calm and effective in your day-to-day life. It turns out, helping your parent brain move through and past life's stressful parenting moments requires thinking and behaving in new, more adaptive ways.

As you read this book and begin to apply new tools and skills in your own life, you will gain enhanced parenting abilities, including (but not limited to):

- Replacing harsh, judgmental self-criticism with supportive self-compassion

- Seeing the world around you through a grounded, realistic lens (rather than a spiraling, worst-case-scenario lens)

- Embracing the present moment and reaping the benefits of mindful parenting

- Moving through and past your own history and life's pain points

- Managing your own (as well as your child's) big emotions

- Embracing the limits of your control and developing greater trust in your child

- Moving toward the things you value most in the midst of your busy, child-centered life

- Being a *good enough* parent in a perfectly imperfect world, rather than striving for unrealistic, perfectionistic parenting

- Experiencing long-term, sustainable emotional well-being

Strengthening your parent brain's mental muscles around these core coping capabilities won't happen by simply reading this book. There *are* some great ideas in these pages, but the true magic happens when you put the concepts into practice. Consider this book more like a membership to a brain gym rather than an invitation to attend a talk.

Throughout this book, you will meet different parents attempting to manage the stressful, anxiety-provoking moments of their lives. Some are stuck in their anxiety; others are practicing one (or more) of these core coping concepts. Each chapter helps you understand what makes these skills so powerful, stress-reducing, and life-enhancing. The rest of the chapter introduces and guides you through targeted exercises to strengthen your brain's neurocircuitry. Rewiring your parent brain to operate more effectively takes targeted practice and action, but it will be transformative. Mental muscles need exercise just like any muscle in the body. The more you activate your effective coping mental circuitry, the stronger those neurological networks become, and the more automatically they will be activated in future stressful scenarios.

We know how difficult it is for busy parents to invest time and energy in themselves. As you take the next step toward more peaceful, joy-filled living, know that your hard work will lead to exponential benefits. It's not only you who will benefit from a less anxious, more serene parent brain—your child has much to gain from this investment in your family. Watch for the "for two" sections where we highlight how the skills you are practicing will give you and your child "two for the price of one" benefits. Thanks to the mirror neurons at play between you and your child (more on this later), when they see you handling life's challenging moments more calmly and effectively, their brain too will begin to rewire itself to manage life's inevitable stressors with enhanced ease. And your child doesn't have to do any work to gain these benefits. No nagging, harassing, or prompting them into more effectively managing the moment. As you work on your own parent brain, their brain will ultimately follow suit. You're embarking on a journey toward positive change not only for yourself, but also for your entire family.

Now it's time to treat yourself and your parent brain to the limitless possibilities of parenting with less stress and anxiety. We hope this book will give you and your family the necessary tools to minimize life's stressful moments and maximize life's moments of joy, connection, and delight. You and your family deserve it.

With immense gratitude to all parents,

Debra Kissen, PhD, MHSA

Micah Ioffe, PhD

Hannah Romain, LCSW

CHAPTER 1

Your Brain on Parenting

Picture baby sea turtles hatching on a sandy beach. Soon the babies find their way to the water and face the task of surviving independently in the ocean. Humans, on the other hand, are much less self-sufficient and entirely dependent on the care of other humans for many, many years. Unlike most other animals, humans are born entirely helpless and in need of around-the-clock caretaking to survive, thrive, and eventually gain self-sufficiency years down the line. Caretaking for a small human (or small humans) is no easy task.

Imagine a company was looking to hire a parent. The job post would be something like:

> *Help wanted. Hours 24/7. No days off. No salary. Employee must freely contribute all personal financial resources. The job entails constant worry, stress, and fatigue, and occasionally feeling like your heart is being ripped out of your chest. Moments of joy are possible, but not guaranteed.*

Would you apply for this position? Put it like this, and many would say no. Yet most humans do become parents. The job of being a parent can be filled with exponential joy, purpose, and indescribable love. At the same time, it can bring overwhelming stress, anxiety, and difficulty. So how do we do it? How do so many humans just like you sign up for this job and actually survive all of the thrills and spills that parenting brings?

Fortunately for the survival of the human race, there are all kinds of emotion-based pulls and drives that guide parents forward and encourage caretaking behaviors. To provide everything parents need to raise little humans, the brain and body are programmed with several physiological mechanisms that encourage highly sensitive attunement and prioritization of children's evolving needs. Most parents have not given much thought to all that goes on in their brain and body to promote their family's well-being (and survival).

But science has pondered this. An innovative line of research has used neuroimaging to examine areas of the parental brain (Squire & Stein, 2003) that enhance bonding and reward selfless over selfish interacting with one's child. The research has highlighted activation of dedicated circuitry, including areas responsible for motivation, reward processing, enhanced memory processing, increased sensitivity to threat cues, and shared experiencing via empathy (Piallini, De Palo, & Simonelli, 2015). Parents' brains actually look different from nonparents'. Your brain is specifically, incredibly wired for parenting.

Feeling for Two

The unique patterns in parent brains show activation by mirror neurons, which enhance motivation to prioritize another person's needs over your own and allow for empathy—one key to all your nurturing and caretaking. If you couldn't feel another's emotions (such as your child's), you could easily disregard them and tend only to your own needs. Mirror neurons fire in response to what others do or feel, leading us to "mirror" their behavior and connect through shared experience. When you cry during a sad movie or laugh along along with someone else's laughter, your mirror neurons are responsible.

Empathy's power has no greater hold on you than in parenting. When your child experiences joy, pain, or any feeling in between, your mirror neurons cause your parent brain to light up in many ways, causing you to feel what they're feeling—your child's physical pain, the devastation of failing a school test, being shunned in the lunch room, or waking up with a high fever. Of course, conversely you can also feel (from your audience seat) your child's incredible joy at their first dance recital or (from the stands) the thrill of making the game-winning shot. Your parent brain allows you to feel their lowest lows and highest highs.

The same mirror neurons that heighten your understanding of your child's inner world also cause your child to take on *your* emotional experience. As your and your child's mirror neurons fire back and forth, you may find yourselves stuck in a feedback loop of emotional distress. Many parents are familiar with the out-of-control experience of feeling as though their child's upset feeds their own upset or vice versa. Your child's emotional distress can increase your emotional distress, which can increase their emotional distress... and round and round you both go.

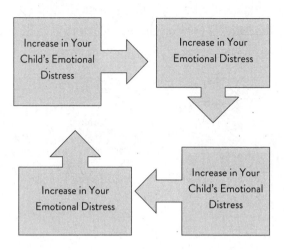

A Prehistoric Parent Brain in a Modern World

The modern parent brain has not evolved much from the days when human children needed protection from roaming predators. Our world has evolved exponentially since then, yet our brains have not changed as quickly. In humanity's early days, parents needed to be on high alert to protect their children from constant environmental threats. While modern living presents new threats to survival, the level of activation and energy required to seek safety from a prehistoric predator is not quite to scale with today's modern parenting challenges. If your child didn't get invited to a birthday party but several of her friends did, it's not life or death. The more evolved part of your brain—your prefrontal cortex (PFC)—understands this. Yet the older, deeper part of your parent brain, the amygdala, interprets the situation as a grave threat to your child's safety and well-being, deserving of serious parental attention.

Human brains around the world experience misfiring and false alarms from the amygdala daily (think of times your stress or anxiety seems disproportionate to a situation). These stress-inducing, anxiety-provoking alarm signals from your brain can be exhausting. Yet one could argue that these safety-focused brain signals are advantageous from a survival standpoint. Sometimes our brain has good reason to sound an alarm.

Imagine swimming with your child in calm water. You see a brown object floating in the distance. Would you rather your brain signaled, *Grab child and flee now. Alligator approaching!* or *Hmm…not sure what that object could be. Why don't you and your child swim over there and take a closer look?*

Even if it turns out to be just a tree branch, most people would argue that those alarm bells are completely worth it, just in case it really *is* an alligator.

While these mental alarm signals are important and necessary for survival, experiencing nonstop, excessive false alarms takes a toll on your emotional well-being and increases your overall stress and anxiety. As parents constantly worry about their children's safety and well-being, they experience emotional distress unique to parents. But just because your parent brain may chronically misfire or send false-alarm signals does not mean you must believe it. The brain rewiring exercises you'll engage in throughout this book will help give your parent brain a twenty-first-century system upgrade, so it can move through modern-day parenting challenges with enhanced ease and efficiency.

Neuroanatomy 101: A Brief Brain Primer

The first step in rewiring your parent brain to operate more effectively is gaining a basic understanding of your brain's multiple operating systems. Just as understanding your muscular system can help you choose strength training exercises, understanding your brain and the neurocircuitry most associated with parenting will help you learn to calm down overactivated brain areas and activate dormant or underused ones.

The human brain's power and information-processing potential are awe inspiring. Its hundreds of billions of neurons (or nerve cells) each have the capacity to interconnect with ten thousand other neurons, all transmitting and processing information at lightning speed. These interconnections (think *wiring*) allow you to fully experience the world around you and to feel, think, and take actions that align with your goals and interests.

Your Brain's Hardware

Different parts of your brain perform different critical functions to maximize your chances of survival and minimize contact with potential threats to you and your loved ones. Some parts are more primitive and similar to other mammals'; others are more evolved, allowing you to plan, predict, and reflect on your experience as only humans can do. The more developed parts allow you to engage in complex thinking and access unique abilities, like language and detailed thought processes. These are essential for survival and have allowed humans to find novel solutions to ever-evolving challenges.

Let's look at four key areas of the human brain and how they interact to create your inner and outer experience.

THE AMYGDALA

Think of your amygdala as your emotional brain; it doesn't think, but feels its way through life. It quickly sizes up a situation and determines whether it is good or bad, safe or dangerous. It takes in information so quickly that it's already decided how it feels before your more rational, thinking brain has begun its fact-based assessment. Your amygdala performs its critical function outside of your conscious awareness. Therefore, while sometimes it's crystal clear to you why you're feeling what you're feeling, other times you experience emotions that don't always make sense to you. For example, you may feel anxious and on edge, sitting in the carpool line waiting to pick up your child from school. While your rational brain knows you are safe and sound in the comfortable seat of a temperature-controlled vehicle, your amygdala may be triggered, fearing the consequences of being late for an after-school activity.

Your amygdala learns through experience. It does not use logic to reach its emotional conclusions, and it is always on high alert for potential danger and constantly reviewing incoming data. When it detects any potential threats, it sends out high alert warnings in your brain, signaling your body to prepare for danger. These are more than a simple *Watch out!*—you can feel the warning throughout your body. Your senses are flooded with the danger message, and your brain is hardwired to override any rational or logical thinking, prioritizing your amygdala's survival-oriented messaging.

Your amygdala comes preprogrammed with sensitivities to certain stimuli that are advantageous to survival, such as fear of large animals, heights, sharp objects, and unfamiliar faces. However, fears can also be learned based on life experiences. For example, if your child reports being bullied by a classmate, your amygdala remembers this experience and reminds you to encourage them to avoid similar situations to prevent additional pain and suffering. This could mean feeling anxious or on edge when you notice your child is around this classmate. If your amygdala generalizes this learned experience to protect you and your child from any related threats, you might feel anxious or on edge when your child starts a new friendship with someone who reminds you of the former bully.

While your amygdala is powerful and hardworking, it lacks attention to detail. It's constantly scanning your environment with broad strokes, not assessing the details, such as *Is this other child teasing playfully or in a mean spirit?* Your amygdala is not concerned with subtleties—it only remembers the pain and suffering associated with your child being made fun of and will continue to signal you to keep them away from any other child who might bully them or cause more pain and suffering.

Having an overly eager amygdala is neither good nor bad. Depending on the situation, it can be either very helpful or very uncomfortable.

Pop Quiz

Read the following situations and select those where it would be helpful to have a trigger-happy, highly activated amygdala:

1. You're crossing the street with your children and a distracted driver blows through a stop sign.

2. You're driving with your children and hear them bickering in the back seat.

3. Your child takes the first few bites of a new food and begins complaining of a tingly, itchy mouth.

4. You take your children out for a fancy, special meal and your distracted son spills his drink all over himself and you (and your brand-new shirt).

If you identified situations 1 and 3 as moments when it is helpful to be on high alert for threats, great work! You recognize that having an amygdala highly attuned to danger is not all good or all bad.

There are times when your amygdala helps you and your loved ones survive and there are times when it sends a false alarm and rapidly transforms you from enjoying the moment to feeling anxious, stressed, or on edge. When your amygdala sounds a false alarm, it can be helpful to call upon your PreFrontal Cortex (PFC) to offer a more thoughtful, reason-based assessment of your current situation. Let us further introduce you to your PFC.

THE PREFRONTAL CORTEX (PFC)

Think of your PFC as your thinking brain, assisting you in planning, organizing, and processing complex information. It sorts through incoming sensory input (what you see, hear, smell, taste, touch) and stored memories to decide how to proceed. It uses this information to attach meaning to situations and create memories, which helps you recognize, interpret, and respond to people, places, and things. The PFC also plays a part in self-reflection, working memory, and perspective-taking abilities.

Your PFC not only helps you navigate your current situation but also can review lessons learned and visualize future situations to maximize the likelihood of successful living. For example, if you are considering sending your child to summer camp, your PFC can process what you've learned about available camp programs and your own memories of attending summer camp as a kid. While this complex information processing is incredibly important, sometimes your PFC's ability to picture all possible outcomes of a future scenario hurts more than it helps. This can leave your amygdala feeling overwhelmed by endless potential threats.

Your PFC and your amygdala each influence the other. So if your amygdala sounds a false alarm, believing danger threatens you or your child, it will initiate your fight-flight-freeze response. When your PFC notes that your amygdala believes there is imminent danger, it starts assessing for potential threats.

THE HIPPOCAMPUS

The hippocampus is known for creating and storing short- and long-term memories. It especially remembers highly emotional moments of your life, whether positive or negative. An intensely emotional experience informs your hippocampus that something important has occurred that must be worth remembering. Your hippocampus is constantly sharing information with your amygdala to maximize the value of prior lessons learned. For example, your hippocampus could send this message to your amygdala: *Remember, the last time you went on a family road trip it was a disaster of nonstop fighting and near-death moments as you attempted to referee arguments while driving.* Your amygdala immediately activates your fight-flight-freeze response to prevent a similar experience in the future. Then your PFC joins in: *That road trip was awful. We need to avoid experiences like that at all costs.*

THE HYPOTHALAMUS

Your hypothalamus regulates the bodily functions essential to survival: thirst, hunger, mood, libido, sleep, and body temperature. It orchestrates the release of hormones, keeping your body's complex functions balanced and stabilized. Your hypothalamus sends signals to release specific hormones into the bloodstream—for example, oxytocin, which plays an important role in compassion and social bonding. Oxytocin increases in mothers to facilitate childbirth and lactation; similar levels increase for fathers as they transition to fatherhood (Gordon et al., 2010). Some have described the release of oxytocin as a "warm and fuzzy" sensation that occurs when you feel close to someone. Think of the feeling you get when you wrap your child in a big hug after a long day. Oxytocin and other chemicals released by the hypothalamus help build close and caring relationships with your children and other loved ones.

Neuroplasticity and Your Ability to Rewire Your Brain

Your brain's ability to adapt and rewire itself is called *neuroplasticity*. Each time you think a thought or engage in a behavior, you alter connections between the neurons in your brain. With each action you take, you rewire your brain to experience stronger connections in some areas and weaker connections in others. With repetition, you can strengthen the connections between the neurons associated with specific thoughts, behaviors, and mental states. So the more frequently you engage in thinking and behavioral patterns, the more likely you will think and act in the same manner in the future. When we say "rewire your brain," we mean it!

Imagine you are hiking through a forest. You can follow a clear, well-groomed trail where the dirt has been packed down and well traveled, or you can forge a new path. Traveling down a new path will likely involve clearing branches, traveling over uneven ground, and other possible hindrances. Which path are you more likely to travel? Unless you are actively looking to make your journey a challenging one, chances are you will choose the path more frequently traveled. The same goes for your brain. It's always looking for opportunities to conserve energy, just as a hiker might conserve energy by taking the well-traveled route. If a situation in your life appears similar to one you've experienced before, your brain is likely to lead you down the path you've been down before. Forging a new path is not an automatic process—you must make an active effort.

As your brain is exposed to new experiences and learns new things, it can reorganize, shift, and change to meet your current and unfolding life requirements. And the more frequently you think a new thought and behave in a new way, the more automatic this novel behavioral repertoire will become. An early study of the brain's ongoing ability to rewire itself was the revolutionary 2000 London Taxi Cab Study. It used MRI technology to compare the brains of seasoned taxi drivers and bus drivers in the city. Bus drivers drive the same route every working day; a taxi driver's route is ever-changing, so they must learn to navigate thousands of different places within the city. The MRIs in this study revealed that the taxi drivers' posterior hippocampi were significantly larger than the bus drivers'. Additionally, the longer someone had been driving a taxi, the larger their hippocampus appeared on the MRI (Maguire et al., 2006). Similar evidence of neuroplasticity can be seen on MRIs of other human brains, such as athletes' or musicians'. Years of musical practice and training can structurally and functionally reorganize the musician's brain (Rodrigues et al., 2010), not unlike the London taxi drivers'. These findings provide incredible evidence of the human brain's neuroplasticity.

The implications of the brain's ability to rewire itself with each new experience is just as relevant for the ever-evolving learning baked into parenting as it is for musicians and taxi drivers. The more frequently you engage in healthy coping in a stressful moment, the more likely you will act effectively in the next similar situation. And of course the reverse is true. The more frequently you lose your cool in the face of a standoff with your child, the more likely you are to act ineffectively in the next similar situation. Let's apply this to a common challenging parenting moment:

You are trying to get your kids to get off their devices and start getting ready for bed. They ignore your prompts, reminders, and warnings. You are feeling hot and frustrated, start to shout, and allow your brain to get sucked into a downward thinking spiral. Then you think about how difficult the kids have been lately, what a terribly ineffective parent you are, and how irritating it is that your partner never steps in for the difficult parenting moments yet always seems to be around for the fun ones.

The next time you face this challenge, you'll likely engage in the same emotionally reactive, self-punishing manner. But let's say you choose to do something different instead. Perhaps you have been reading this book and are working on rewiring your brain to operate more effectively. Instead of choosing the well-traveled path, you:

1. Remind yourself you are about to experience a stressful moment, but you and your family are perfectly fine and not in danger.

2. Select an emotion regulation skill to calm yourself down right before giving them their final warning.

3. Practice coping your way through the kids' whines and complaints without giving in or losing your temper.

By applying new thoughts and behaviors to a familiar situation, you're more likely to think and act in this new, more adaptive way the next time you face the same obstacle. Thanks to neuroplasticity and your brain's lifelong ability to evolve and create new neural connections, healthier, more effective ways of thinking and living are possible.

Welcome to Your Brain Gym

Think of this book as your brain gym. As you create new neural connections, you can choose how to think, feel, and behave rather than automatically veering down the path stress and anxiety have forged for you over time. The exercises you'll engage in throughout the book will help you rewire your parent brain to think, feel, and behave more calmly and effectively.

With practice, you will rewire your brain to more easily move through and past common stressful parenting moments. It's much like the work needed to learn and master physical skills—even people born with advanced athletic abilities must train to achieve peak performance. To feel calm, cool, and collected as a parent takes ongoing commitment to your mental fitness. You've already picked up this book and read this far, which is a testament to your ability to do this challenging, important, and transformative work. We are so glad that you are on this journey. You and your family deserve it.

Cognitive Behavioral Therapy to Rewire Your Parent Brain

All of the brain rewiring exercises you will engage in here are derived from cognitive behavioral therapy (CBT). CBT is considered the gold standard, primary therapeutic treatment for adults with mild to moderate symptoms of stress and anxiety—although for more severe symptoms of anxiety, research suggests that a combination of CBT and medication is most effective (Geller & March, 2012; Koran et al., 2007).

CBT is an action-oriented, evidence-based approach to treatment, based on the idea that thoughts, feelings, and behaviors are interconnected. Your thoughts affect how you feel and what you do (or avoid doing), your feelings affect what you think and do, and your behaviors affect what you think and how you feel.

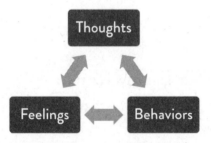

Therefore, what you tell yourself or believe about a situation affects how you feel and the actions you ultimately decide to take. Sometimes problems arise when unhelpful ways of thinking and ineffective behavioral patterns take over. When this happens, CBT can help improve thinking, feeling, and behavior patterns to promote living life to the fullest.

Before you begin using your new brain gym membership, we recommend you gather a few items—and, more important, take some time to harness the motivation and energy you will need to engage in this important work. The goal is to set yourself up for success. Taking the time for planning up front can be the difference between true progress and disappointment or feelings of failure. It's kind of like wanting to get fit but never planning time in your day to get to the gym for a workout. So let's take a moment to get you set up for success.

Getting Started

To get the most out of the parent brain rewiring exercises, we recommend you devote a journal or notebook to exclusively use as your *Brain Rewiring Training Journal*. You will see this symbol 📓 when you need your journal to complete an activity or consider a reflection question. It is helpful to document your experience with each exercise and write your answers to reflection questions so you can access this material later.

Some of our clients would rather walk on hot coals than have to track their work by hand using pen and paper. If you feel similarly, we recommend creating a web-based document to dedicate to this work—one that you can easily access at all times. Some of our clients even prefer to use the "Notes" section of their phone. Use whatever information tracking method works best for you and your lifestyle. The most important thing is that you are realistic with yourself: What format will make it easiest for you to consistently complete the exercises in this book and track your progress?

Additionally, throughout this book you will see the icon ♔. This means that free tools—worksheets and examples—are available to download at http://www.newharbinger.com/50300 to help you complete the exercise.

Your Balanced Parenting Scorecard: The Before Snapshot

It is time for a baseline assessment of your parent brain's strengths and challenge zones. Getting a clear picture of your strengths, challenges, and vulnerabilities as a parent might feel intimidating or uncomfortable, but it is a worthwhile and impactful step toward creating the change you seek. With a comprehensive understanding of how your brain currently operates "on parenting," you can start to identify clear, actionable goals to work toward, as you move through this book and beyond.

Take a moment to think about this past week. On a scale of 0 to 10 (with 0 being not at all and 10 being very much so), rate the extent to which you agree with each of the following statements:

Self-Compassion

1. I strive to be self-compassionate rather than self-critical.

2. I can recognize when I am stuck in self-judgment and not working toward finding a solution to improve my situation.

3. I can notice myself having a self-critical thought without believing that judgment represents truth.

4. I can shift from beating myself up to more effective problem solving.

5. I can compassionately guide myself through stressful situations.

Total Self-Compassion score: _____

Realistic Thinking

1. I can notice when my mind is stuck in negative thinking mode.

2. When I am stuck in a negative thinking loop, I can disengage from these thoughts and bring my attention back to the present moment.

3. When I find myself worrying about my child's well-being, I can evaluate the situation logically, rather than emotionally.

4. I feel equipped to challenge unhelpful worry thoughts so I can stay in the moment with my family.

5. I can distinguish between a true problem to be solved and general life uncertainty to be tolerated.

Total Realistic Thinking score: _____

Mindfulness

1. I can fully engage in the present moment when I spend time with my children.

2. I can listen and actually hear what my child is expressing as we talk.

3. I feel connected to my child as we engage in activities together.

4. Throughout the day, I can notice distracting mental noise and then gently bring my attention back to the current moment.

5. Even during times of high anxiety and stress, I can remain present with my family.

Total Mindfulness score: _____

Freedom from Your Past

1. I can experience reminders of painful moments from my childhood without becoming overwhelmed or avoidant.

2. Difficult moments from my past do not prevent me from living a full life in the present.

3. I can separate the difficult moments I had in my childhood from my fears and concerns for my children.

4. When my child is feeling emotional pain or distress, I can believe in their resilience, rather than feel triggered and overwhelmed by the need to rescue them.

5. I can differentiate between when I am truly in danger and when my brain is experiencing a false alarm.

Total Freedom from Your Past score: _____

Emotional Regulation

1. I can calm myself down and cool off my emotional temperature when I feel stressed, frustrated, or anxious.

2. During stressful parenting moments I can take the time to first calm myself down and then choose how to proceed, rather than letting my emotional reactions call the shots.

3. I am aware of and can predict which parenting situations are most likely to stress me out and cause me to feel out of control.

4. I proactively plan for how I will try to calm myself down in common stressful parenting situations.

5. I am proud of how I model self-regulation for my children, even during life's stressful moments.

Total Emotional Regulation score: _____

Limits of Control

1. I strive to choose my battles with my child carefully, based on our family values and the aspects of life that are nonnegotiable.

2. I can recognize when my attempts at controlling the uncontrollable are backfiring, causing tension in my relationship with my child.

3. I understand and accept that as much as I care about my child and want to protect them from experiencing any harm or suffering, there is only so much I can control about how their life will unfold.

4. I strive to reserve my parenting energy for maximizing meaningful interactions with my child rather than attempting to control my child.

5. I believe in my child's resilience and ability to handle life's obstacles, even if their path forward is not exactly the same path I would have chosen for them.

Total Limits of Control score: _____

Valued Living

1. Making time for myself and my own needs is a priority in my life.

2. I can give time and attention to my children's activities and interests, while also giving time and attention to my own activities and interests.

3. I strive to engage in behaviors and activities that align with my values and priorities.

4. Every day I make the time to reenergize with moments (big or small) of relaxation, enjoyment, or connection with something I truly care about.

5. My child (or other family members) could tell you what my personal values and interests are.

Total Valued Living score: _____

Perfectly Imperfect Parenting

1. I am an imperfect parent, and that is okay with me.

2. When faced with a seemingly impossible parenting to-do, I can take small action steps to address the situation, instead of avoiding due to fear of messing up or being judged.

3. I am allowed to make mistakes.

4. I accept "good enough" living over perfection, which leaves me with more time to be present and enjoy the moment with my family.

5. I know that doing my best (whatever my best may look like on any given day) is good enough for myself, my partner, and my children.

Total Perfectly Imperfect Parenting score: _____

Your Balanced Parenting Scorecard Before Snapshot

Balanced Parenting Skill	Total Score (0–50)
Self-Compassion	
Realistic Thinking	
Mindfulness	
Freedom from Your Past	
Emotional Regulation	
Limits of Control	
Valued Living	
Perfectly Imperfect Parenting	

Understanding Your Results

If your total Self-Compassion score is:

0–20: You deserve a whole lot more of this important capability.

21–40: You are doing a good job of offering yourself self-compassion, but you deserve even more of it!

41–50: You are nailing the ability to offer yourself self-compassion instead of getting stuck shaming and blaming yourself about parenting mishaps and mistakes.

If your total Realistic Thinking score is:

0–20: You deserve a whole lot more of this important capability.

21–40: You are doing a good job of thinking realistically rather than catastrophically, but you deserve even more moments experiencing life from this perspective!

41–50: You are nailing the ability to move through stressful parenting moments with a realistic rather than catastrophic mindset.

If your total Mindfulness score is:

0–20: You deserve a whole lot more of this important capability.

21–40: You are doing a good job of living life in the here and now, but you deserve even more moments experiencing life from this perspective!

41–50: You are nailing the ability to live life mindfully, fully present in the here and now.

If your total Freedom from Your Past score is:

0–20: You deserve a whole lot more of this important capability.

21–40: You are doing a good job of not letting pain and suffering from your past get in the way of living life to the fullest, but you deserve even more moments experiencing life from this perspective!

41–50: You are nailing the ability to move through prior times of pain and suffering, allowing you to live your current life to the fullest.

If your total Emotional Regulation score is:

0–20: You deserve a whole lot more of this important capability.

21–40: You are doing a good job of calming yourself down when you are feeling stressed and anxious, but you deserve even more of the ability to regulate your emotional temperature!

41–50: You are nailing the ability to regulate your emotional temperature and model for your child how to move from feeling out of control and emotionally reactive to feeling calm and grounded.

If your total Limits of Control score is:

0–20: You deserve a whole lot more of this important capability.

21–40: You are doing a good job of understanding where your control over your child stops and their self-control starts, but you deserve even more of the ability to direct your emotional energy toward strengthening your connection and sharing moments of joy with your child.

41–50: You are nailing the ability to pick your battles and know when to try to control your child and when to believe in their resilience and ability to handle aspects of life on their own terms.

If your total Valued Living score is:

0–20: You deserve a whole lot more of this important capability.

21–40: You are doing a good job of differentiating between who you are as a parent and who you are on a broader level, but you deserve even more moments to engage with the things that energize and revitalize you most.

41–50: You are nailing the ability to fulfill your role as a parent while also maintaining your own values and cultivating the aspects of your life that inspire, energize, and fill you up the most.

If your total Perfectly Imperfect Parenting score is:

0–20: You deserve a whole lot more of this important capability.

21–40: You are doing a good job of accepting that to be human is to make occasional mistakes, but you deserve even more moments of perfectly imperfect living.

41–50: You are nailing the ability to take chances, learn through doing, and model perfectly imperfect living for your child.

 Next, map out your Balanced Parenting Graphical Scorecard Before Snapshot on the worksheet available to download at (www.newharbinger .com/50300).

Hold onto this *before* snapshot of your balanced parenting capabilities. Try not to read too much into your score or place judgment on it. No matter your score, you are taking wonderful, worthwhile steps toward becoming a more grounded, effective parent, and this is only the beginning. We will revisit this data in chapter 10 when you will have the opportunity to take your *after* snapshot.

What Motivates You to Do This Work?

You can rewire your brain to respond less anxiously and more effectively to stressful parenting moments by *repeatedly* practicing thinking and behaving in new, more adaptive ways. But it can be hard to muster the emotional energy required to bring about change. Your brain is used to doing things the way it has most frequently done them in the past. It's easier and feels more comfortable to stick with what you know, because your brain's default mode is to take the strongest, most familiar neural pathway. Just as hikers create the well-worn central groove in the trail, your every engagement in the same parental behavioral repertoire makes your brain more likely to respond that way in the future. Actively choosing to forge a new path takes extra effort up front. But soon enough this new path will also become well worn, and eventually it will be just as easy to travel it. By strengthening neural pathways associated with calm, effective parenting, your brain will more automatically activate these more adaptive thoughts, feelings, and behaviors.

Parent Brain Rewiring Exercise: Your Parenting Magic Wand

This is a reflective journaling exercise. You'll need five to ten uninterrupted minutes to write your answers to the following reflection questions in your Training Journal.

- If you had a magic wand and on the count of three—poof!—you were no longer struggling with parenting stress and anxiety, how would your life look different?

- What would you be doing at this very moment (besides not reading this book)?

- What activities would you be engaging in?

- What are you missing out on because of the time and energy you spend feeling stressed, anxious, worried, and/or overwhelmed?

- What aspects of life do you value the most, and how much time in your current life are you spending engaging in them?

Here's how one of our parent clients completed this exercise:

If I had a magic wand and could drastically decrease the amount of parenting stress and anxiety I experience, the first thing that comes to mind is that I would be more present in my daily life. If I wasn't so chronically overwhelmed, I would be able to sit down for dinner with my family and really listen and share in the laughter and conversation at the table instead of being consumed by my own thoughts. I would have more time to spend with my children instead of encouraging them to play without me because I'm "too stressed" to spend that time with them. I might even be more able to trust that my kids can handle what comes their way, rather than spending so much energy trying to shield them from the less-than-ideal parts of life. Less anxiety and stress would also allow me to be a better version of myself in my relationship with my husband. Instead of my being in my head and worrying about things that haven't happened yet, we could spend more time together chatting and unwinding at the end of the day like we used to. If my parenting stress was minimized, I would feel more at peace and more able to move through the obstacles that our family faces from time to time, rather than feeling paralyzed or spiraling when challenges do arise. I know life with less stress and anxiety wouldn't be without challenges, but it would mean more peace and more joy.

How This Exercise Is Rewiring Your Parent Brain

Your parent brain needs encouragement to invest your energy in this brain rewiring work rather than going with your familiar thinking and parenting patterns. By engaging in this exercise, you were able to jump-start the rewiring process and solidify your motivation. There may be times, as you move through this training program, that your brain will protest this work. In those moments, have this exercise handy to remind yourself of your goals and desires, and to help you visualize what your life can and will be once you train your parent brain to operate with greater ease.

A Moment for Reflection

Recall why you chose to pick up this book and start reading in the first place. Remind yourself how far you have come and what possibilities lie ahead.

CHAPTER 2

The Power of Self-Compassion for Parents

We begin this chapter with a story of two parents. You may recognize the challenges they each faced with a new baby—and their responses.

Diego and Mark were best friends since high school and moved through all the same life stages together. They both started their first full-time job after college, proposed to their spouses within six months of each other, and tragically lost a parent in their thirties. Diego and Mark were always there for each other, relying on each other's support and friendship through each life transition. It wasn't surprising that their firstborn children arrived and both men became fathers within just two months of each other. They had nervously joked about their upcoming adventures as a parent, making light of the fact that they had no clue what to expect. Diego was the first to experience fatherhood, while Mark anxiously observed the ups and downs of caring for a newborn through his best friend's eyes.

When Diego's son was first born, he told Mark all about the emotional roller coaster of being a new parent. Not yet having his own child, Mark sensed his distress and offered support to Diego in his new role of Dad. Mark could easily understand why his friend felt distressed—there were no user manuals for being a parent! He told Diego not to be so hard on himself: "It's supposed to be a wild ride—this is uncharted territory for us, and I'll be in the same boat soon." However, when it was Mark's turn to step into the Dad role, he found himself floundering.

During the first month, each father struggled to adjust to their new reality. They had almost no time for themselves, and it seemed that all other priorities had disappeared. Caring for their infants was now their full-time job. They planned to catch up whenever they would finally have a moment. As with past experiences, they bonded over new parenting challenges: nonstop crying, failed attempts to comfort, cycling through continual feeding and diaper changes, no showers, no relaxing, no sleep. It was a completely new life milestone, unlike any other.

While Mark knew they were both learning the ropes, he was stuck on the intense discomfort he felt when his baby cried. How were parents supposed to know what their baby needed to make them stop crying? It felt like nothing he tried would work. He desperately sought answers from Diego. To Mark's disappointment, Diego had no quick fixes. In fact, he had no solutions at all. He did exactly what Mark had already been doing: trying out any and all options to comfort his infant.

Mark's Parent Brain Default State: Shame and Blame

Mark felt consumed by thoughts of failure. He doubted his ability to parent, provide for, and comfort his newborn daughter. He often blamed himself for not doing the "right thing" and not knowing what exactly his daughter needed. Feelings of frustration, shame, and guilt sat with him for most of the day. He was his own worst critic. His parent brain offered up thoughts such as You should know what to do—what's wrong with you? Every other parent has figured it out! and You don't even know what she needs! What kind of parent are you? Even though he could logically see that these criticisms weren't necessarily true, he could not shake off the feeling of shame. With every cry from his daughter, his heart pounded, his chest felt heavy, and his mind raced. He ran around trying everything to soothe her. His mind was stuck in a battle between Hurry up and find a solution and What's the point? You suck at this parenting thing anyway. He soon felt defeated, discouraged, and just plain exhausted. In these challenging moments, Mark struggled to offer himself the same support and encouragement that he had so easily provided to Diego.

Diego's Parent Brain Default State: Self-Compassion

Diego also shared Mark's frustration with constant infant cries and failed attempts to comfort. Every ear-piercing scream gave him a painful stab of guilt and a strong urge to calm his son. He noticed a rush of panic and anxiety when he was unable to "just figure it out," as Mark had assumed. Diego heard the whisperings of his inner critic start to creep in, blaming him for not properly tending to his son's needs: Do you even know what you're doing? *Although tempted, Diego did not buy into these thoughts of shame and blame. He noticed his mind offering up this unhelpful and untrue perspective. Then he offered himself the same encouragement he had recently received from Mark. He reminded himself that even though this felt immensely uncomfortable, it was a normal part of the parenting journey. Without shame and blame weighing him down, Diego could use his mental energy to effectively think through possible solutions.*

Diego's pivot from shame and blame to self-compassion did not come easily. It required the work of noticing when his parent brain was offering up unfair criticism rather than helpful encouragement. He actively practiced offering himself the same kindness and understanding for navigating new situations that he had offered to Mark: This is hard, and it's perfectly okay and normal to feel overwhelmed—I've never done this before, and I can handle it. *With compassion for himself, Diego was better able to tolerate and embrace the daily uncertainty of being a new parent.*

These first-time fathers wanted to be the best parents they could be. They shared a strong desire to comfort and provide for their children—now and in the future. By enhancing his self-compassion capabilities, Mark was more easily able to manage, problem solve, and find delight in this new life terrain he was attempting to navigate.

From Shame and Blame to Self-Compassion

You have likely encountered similar challenges in raising your child. Your parent brain may have immediately offered up a variation of *Why aren't you doing this right?!* It may have pulled you into the cycle of blaming yourself for challenges instead of recognizing that this challenge is a normal and expected part of the parenting experience. But you can rewire your parent brain to shift from punitive taskmaster to encouraging coach by upgrading your intrapersonal communication skills and tools.

This chapter will help you learn to:

- Recognize when your brain is stuck in an unhelpful, ineffective shame-and-blame cycle

- Dial down its generation of self-critical thoughts and increase its ability to engage in effective problem solving

- Learn to serve as a compassionate coach and guide you through parenting challenges with increased support and decreased punitive messaging

Your Parent Brain in Shame-and-Blame Mode

Why is it so easy for your brain to spew self-blame and judgment? Is there be something wrong with you if you engage in this kind of thinking so frequently? It is *not* just you. We humans are hardwired to prioritize survival over peace of mind. Your brain is *supposed* to notify you when it detects something that feels wrong, whether internally or externally. In uncertain or challenging situations, your quick-to-protect parent brain may flood you with self-criticism, shame, and blame in hopes that you'll retreat from any situation that may threaten you or your loved ones. Your parent brain in shame-and-blame mode operates in the same state of threat detection as it does when it notes external danger—but the threat it detects is *you*. When a self-critical thought arises, your amygdala detects the "threat" and activates your hypothalamus, releasing stress hormones as it prepares to fight. Your hippocampus scours its collection of memories for what may have protected you or hurt you in the past. This primitive fight-flight-freeze response is not helpful for motivating corrective action and the creative thinking necessary to navigate complex parenting terrain.

Some people can rapidly and seamlessly shift gears and transition from problem recognition to problem-solving mode. Others tend to:

1. Detect something that feels wrong, internally or externally.

2. Beat themself up and review all the ways this could have or should have been prevented.

3. Eventually reroute back to problem-solving mode after using excess energy and time stuck in a shame-and-blame loop.

Both your genetics and early life experiences lay the groundwork for how easily your parent brain may either (1) efficiently transition to problem-solving mode when facing a challenge or (2) get stuck in shame and blame before returning to the task at hand and determining how to proceed. You may be genetically hardwired to have a strong negative emotional reaction to anything you view as a preventable mistake. Or you may have grown up in an environment where it felt dangerous to make mistakes. You may have learned that the emotional discomfort of getting things wrong is unbearable. You may have promised yourself to always do everything in your power to be perfect and not risk being on the receiving end of punishing words or behaviors.

When your parent brain is in shame-and-blame mode, it holds you responsible for any and all problems in your life. It's trying (but failing) to protect you from any other potentially painful situations by loudly alerting you to your past, current, and future mistakes. While it is helpful for your parent brain to offer you course-correction prompts such as *Pay attention; your son needs extra support with school*, shame-and-blame thoughts like *It's your fault he's failing math—you never pay enough attention to your children* are rarely helpful and always painful. Once you enter shame-and-blame mode, it's easy to start questioning additional aspects of yourself, like your abilities and decisions, and soon you're trapped in a pit of self-doubt. When bombarded with self-generated propaganda about just how incompetent and terrible you are, you have even less energy and mental space to focus on the unsolved problem that set off the shame-and-blame alert in the first place. But you can rewire your parent brain, enhancing your ability to easily, efficiently shift from problem detection to problem solving. As you practice the exercises throughout this chapter, you will be creating deeper mental grooves in the pathway from problem recognition to problem solving. With continued daily practice you will feel less pulled into repeatedly reminding yourself of all of the terrible things you have done in your life and all the ways you have "messed up" that have led you to any less-than-ideal situation.

Self-Compassion for Two

As you begin opening up to the possibility of practicing self-compassion, note that practicing *self*-compassion as a parent has benefits far beyond yourself. Practicing self-compassion can also have an amazingly positive impact on your child's mental and emotional well-being. Each time you practice self-compassion, you model this behavior for your child—teaching them that they, just like you, are worthy of being treated with care, respect, and understanding. Even more so, you show them that these can come from within. Rather than modeling self-blame and shame, you can teach your child a more adaptive way of being that will serve them for their entire life.

While you are certainly welcome to talk with your child about self-compassion, you can actually teach them about this practice without a lecture or lengthy explanation. When your child witnesses you acting with self-compassion, mirror neurons will fire in response to what they are witnessing, leading them to mirror your emotions and behaviors. Of course, this same process can also work for blame and shame. When your child observes you engaging in self-blame and shame, their brain takes in this information too. When it comes to self-compassion, the best thing you can do for your child is practice it for yourself. Think about how you would like your child to be treated when they make a mistake or are faced with a challenge, and practice treating yourself in that way. As your child observes this, they are more likely to treat themself with the same self-compassion.

Parent Brain Rewiring Exercise: Getting to Know Your Shame-and-Blame Story

We all have a shame-and-blame story. This is what your parent brain tells you about yourself when it determines you may have made a mistake or gotten something wrong. This five-part exercise will take about twenty minutes; you will need your Training Journal.

1. The following are common thoughts parents have about their own shame-and-blame stories. Note if any are a part of your story. See if you can add some more:

    *   There must be something wrong with me.
    *   I am not a _____ (good, supportive, and so on) enough parent.
    *   I am just as _____ (bad, lazy, and so on) as my own parent.
    *   I will never be the type of parent I want to be.
    *   I can't handle life; I must not be parent material.
    *   It's all my fault that my kids are struggling.
    *   What kind of example am I setting for my kids?
    *   Why can't I just be normal like other parents?
    *   I'm a bad parent (and/or spouse, friend, coworker, and so on).
    *   I am a disaster, a pathetic and anxious mess.
    *   I will never live up to others' expectations.
    *   I am not strong enough to be a parent.
    *   I am broken; I will never be okay.

2. How much of your life is impacted by self-blame? When you are struggling, which areas of your life does your parent brain tend to readily bring up? Write down the loudest self-critical thought your brain offers you in each area.

    *   Parenting
    *   Romantic relationships
    *   Relationships with your parents or family of origin
    *   Friendships
    *   Work and career
    *   Past experiences and future goals

3. You have probably been hearing these thoughts for a long time—it's an old story.

    *   When did you begin hearing this story?

- Has it been the same old story all along? Or has the content ebbed and flowed with your life experiences?

- Can you find a main theme to your story? For instance, does your self-criticism always try to convince you that you are never enough? What is your self-criticism trying to protect you from?

4. What is a more accurate, helpful, and kind story about yourself? Approach it with curiosity. Write this in your Training Journal.

New Story: *I make mistakes—I'm human. I don't always mess up; I have accomplished many things. I can learn from my mistakes and guide my child to learn as I keep doing. I don't have to take my thoughts so seriously. So thanks, parent brain, for that familiar shame-and-blame story, but it's getting old.*

- What did you notice about your experience writing your new story? Reflect on new thoughts, feelings, physical sensations, or urges to take action.

- Was it difficult to reframe your old story? Did you notice that it was tough to let go or see your old story as untrue or unhelpful?

Common Myths of Self-Criticism and Blame

If we could magically get your parent brain to stop beating you up, would you take us up on it? Many clients we work with are quick to say yes. They describe how bad it feels to be on the receiving end of self-criticism and how desperately they want to eliminate this ineffective thinking style. But when we talk further, some become hesitant. They begin to recognize their fears of letting go of self-criticism. They are concerned about becoming too complacent or lazy. They're not sure how else they will create change if they stop beating themselves up.

Common misconceptions associated with beating yourself up are that it will:

- Encourage effective action

- Keep you from being complacent and accepting the status quo

- Be a deserved punishment for your past mistakes

- Remind you of your mistakes so you can avoid repeating them

Research demonstrates that self-criticism does just the opposite. Beating yourself up serves only to consume brain resources that you could otherwise use to effectively address problems. Self-criticism can actually (1) impair your ability to come up with effective solutions and (2) reduce your confidence in taking action (Covert et al., 2003). As your inner critic detects something wrong within, your parent brain becomes more reactive to other potential threats. The rest of your nervous system follows, with increased blood pressure, heightened adrenaline, and a rush of cortisol (the primary stress hormone). Not only is this activated physical state highly uncomfortable, but it is also unproductive and consumes your body and mind energy you could otherwise devote to problem solving or valued living. Operating in shame and blame mode keeps you overwhelmed with feelings of anxiety and fear, preventing you from effectively moving through your many parenting challenges.

Beating yourself up serves no purpose; it only exacerbates your stress and anxiety. What *will* help you move forward and engage in effective problem solving is becoming a realistic, authentic, and helpful coach for yourself.

Parent Brain Rewiring Exercise: What Keeps Your Old Shame-and-Blame Story Going?

 Review these common misconceptions about self-blame. In your Training Journal, take a moment to note which misconceptions have felt true to you in the past.

If I keep criticizing myself...

- I can be a more effective parent.

- I can avoid making the same mistakes in the future.

- It will keep me motivated—otherwise, I might settle for status quo parenting.

- My laziness/other undesirable characteristics will lessen.

- I will raise my children in the best possible way.

- I will push myself to do better or more.

- I will be punishing myself for past mistakes.

- It will force me to make a change.

- I'll live up to everyone's expectations.

- No one else can hurt me with their criticism.

Reflection Questions

1. Which reasons tend to fuel your shame-and-blame patterns?

   - Are they true? Are they always effective?

   - How does it make you feel? Would you offer this reason to your child? A friend?

2. What is your parent brain trying to protect you from?

   - Is it working? If yes, at what cost? If not, it's time to try something else.

Critical Coaching versus Compassionate Coaching

Let's return to Diego's story:

Diego was having a rough start to his work day. He had barely slept, because his son was up for most of the night. And of course today was the day he had to lead a meeting with his boss for the CEO of his company. He told himself he would just do his best and hoped his performance would not be impacted by his less-than-ideal mental state. After the meeting, Diego knew that while it went okay, he had led better meetings in the past. Diego's boss called and immediately laid into him. He asked if there was something wrong with him and questioned his commitment to the project and his team. His boss angrily reminded Diego that he had other managers to

coach who would not be wasting his time. He ended by informing Diego
that with his lack of preparedness he would not be earning a promotion
anytime soon.

Take a moment to reflect on Diego's experience.

- How do you think Diego is feeling as his boss berates him?

- How motivated do you think Diego is to do a good job?

- How confident do you think Diego is feeling?

- How strong and capable do you think Diego is feeling?

- How likely is it that Diego will do well the next time he has to lead an important meeting with his critical boss?

Parent Brain Rewiring Exercise: Is Criticism Working for You?

Use your Training Journal to write down your answers to these questions.

Think of a time in your own life when someone coached you or spoke to you in a harsh, aggressive fashion.

- How did it make you feel?

- How motivated for success were you after this interaction?

Now think of a time when someone coached you in an encouraging, supportive manner.

- How did it make you feel?

- How motivated for success were you after this interaction?

How is beating yourself up going? Is it working? Is it helping you be a better parent? Is it allowing you more time with your child? Is it giving you more emotional energy—or less?

Are you ready to try something else?

Parent Brain Rewiring Exercise: Critical Coach versus Compassionate Coach

By becoming a more educated and astute observer of your thoughts, you can choose which thinking patterns to enhance and which to phase out, depending on how they serve you in living life on your terms. Creating some distance between yourself and your thoughts will make it easier to choose whose advice you would rather listen to.

In your Training Journal, consider why it might be time to retire your old critical coach and welcome your compassionate coach. Reflect on the following questions:

Retire Your Old Critical Coach (we all have one)

- *Who* is your Critical Coach? (Give it a name and describe what it might look like.)

- *What* does it tell you? (List two of its common thoughts or beliefs.)

- *Why* does it do that? (Because of past pain, for protection, to "motivate" you to change?)

- *When* does it scold you? (List any triggers, emotional states, or settings in which you hear it most.)

- *How* does it talk to you? (Describe its tone, wording, images, or flashback memories of pain or failure it throws at you).

Meet Your Compassionate Coach (we all can cultivate one)

- *Who* is your Compassionate Coach? (Give it a name and describe what it might look like.)

- *What* does it have you say to other people when they are struggling? (List how you support your friends and family.)

- *Why* does it have you do that? (Because of past experiences, caring for others, wanting to be helpful?)

- *When* does it support others? (List any times, emotional states, or settings.)

- *How* does it talk to others? (Describe its tone, wording, images, or flashback memories.)

- Does your Compassionate Coach show up only for other people, or does it also show up for you?

For the next week, tune in to your thoughts and notice who is running the show—your old, rude Critical Coach or your realistic, encouraging Compassionate Coach? You might notice your Compassionate Coach mostly tending to the people around you, but nowhere to be found when you yourself face a difficult moment. When you notice the critical one running the show, try to playfully call it out: *Oh, thanks for showing up again, Critical Coach, but your services are no longer required.* See if you can next envision your Compassionate Coach taking its place and providing *you* with the same encouragement it does for others.

From Shame and Blame to Self-Compassion-Infused Problem Solving

What is the first thing that comes to mind when you think of being more compassionate with yourself? For some it elicits a response similar to that of a young child being told to eat their vegetables. We may know being more compassionate to ourself is the "right" thing to do, but it still seems annoying and unappealing. It may feel hokey and pointless. But rewiring your brain to become more self-compassionate is actually the secret to moving past stress and anxiety. By teaching your parent brain how to accept your humanity rather than revolt against it, you will spend so much less time and energy fighting against what is and instead have more of your life force available to craft and live out your best life. Plus, by kindly and respectfully relating and responding to yourself, you will serve as a wonderful model for your child.

The mental health benefits of self-compassion are bountiful: less anxiety and stress, more resilience and optimism. And it has a real positive effect on your brain and body. There are physiological differences between engaging in self-compassion and self-criticism. When you take a more gentle, self-compassionate approach, you reduce opportunities for anxiety and panic to be triggered in your amygdala. A recent study found that when presented with a painful stimulus, individuals with higher self-compassion demonstrated lower activity in the PFC (specifically the dorsolateral prefrontal cortex, or DLPFC [Liu et al., 2020]). This lower level of reactivity in the PFC demonstrates that when using self-compassion, the brain does not have to work as hard to process pain. Self-compassion can help counter self-criticism and foster more mindful, grounded processing of emotional experiences, including pain. Recent research also notes the role of the hypothalamus, with decreases in cortisol (the fight-flight-freeze hormone) and increases in oxytocin (the "love, cuddle, and bonding" hormone) levels when we engage in self-compassion (Rockliff et al., 2008; Wang et al., 2019). When you give yourself kindness and understanding rather than shame and blame, your body reaps the benefits of lowered stress and easier thinking.

You already know how to be compassionate. The average person has more experience offering an accepting, caring attitude to the suffering of others than they are able to apply to their own challenges. Your parent brain has likely offered compassionate responses to your child when they made a mistake or were learning something new. Think back to what you might have told them if they made an error as they were learning to read. We're guessing you didn't offer them a big dose of shame and blame through critical commentary such as "What's wrong with you? You're so dumb. Why is it taking you so long to learn to read? Everyone else is so much better at reading than you. You are never going to make it in life." (Although you probably offer *yourself* self-judgment and harsh criticism when you make a parenting mistake such as showing up at the wrong time for an event or forgetting to get a form in on time.) By enhancing your awareness of how you respond to your loved one's struggles, it can help you tap in to your innate ability to communicate understanding and kindness rather than shame and blame.

Parent Brain Rewiring Exercise: What Would You Tell Your Friend's Parent Brain?

When was the last time you made a parenting mistake? You might have angrily snapped at your teenager, or completely spaced and forgotten about carpool duty. Now imagine that a good friend (a fellow parent) had encountered the same problem. You would probably not call out any "user errors" for them. It is much easier to provide kindness and understanding for others than for ourselves. See Mark's answers to the exercise for an example.

Parenting Mistake: I forgot to buy baby wipes when I was at the store today. Now I need to head back out.

Automatic Response to Myself: Ugh. I always forget something. Why can't I ever just get it right?

Compassionate Response to Diego: Listen, we're functioning on no sleep, and this is new to us. I've also had times where I've messed up the bedtime routine. I know you'll get into a rhythm with things. You got this.

Using the following format as a guide, outline in your Training Journal a recent parenting mistake you made, your automatic response, and the compassionate response you would offer a friend who made the same error.

Parenting Mistake: _____

Automatic Response to Myself: _____

Compassionate Response to a Friend: _____

In your Training Journal, highlight your answer to "Compassionate Response to a Friend." For the next week, for every parenting mishap that arises, use this response as a model to respond to yourself. With each parenting challenge, speak to yourself as though you were offering a good friend the same level of understanding. Notice the overall level of parenting stress and anxiety you feel prior to engaging in this week of forced self-compassion and compare it with how you feel after a week of working your "be accepting and kind to yourself" mental muscles.

Parent Brain Rewiring Exercise: Your Compassionate Coaching Mantra

Consider these compassionate coaching mantras our wonderful clients have found to be helpful:

- Yeah, this sucks, and I know it won't last forever.

- I can move forward with my plan, even with all the anxiety here.

- Thanks, parent brain! I'll let you know when I need some more berating. For now, I'll keep doing my thing.

- This is hard for me because it's brand new; I'll get the hang of it eventually.

- Ugh. This hurts. I know everyone feels pain, and I can work through it.

- I can trust my decisions, feel anxious, and be the parent I want to be.

- Being a parent is hard work. I'm not alone.

- Everyone makes mistakes. I choose to learn from mine.

- I'm feeling pain right now; that is normal. But I don't have to suffer through it.

- This is a tough moment—temporary, difficult, and conquerable.

- "Thank you. Next!" Moving right along, I'll keep doing what is important to me and my family.

Which ones resonate with you? Can you come up with your own? Add them to your Training Journal. Remember to include key components of self-compassion: kindness, understanding, freedom from judgment, present-moment focus, and relating to the common human experience.

Write down each of your top three compassionate coaching mantras on a sticky note. Stick these in places around your home for helpful visual cues to call up your inner Compassionate Coach. We recommend your bathroom mirror, work desk, bedside table, or any other place where you spend time.

Parent Brain Rewiring Exercise: The Self-Compassion Formula

Use this step-by-step guide as you learn and practice authentic self-compassion:

1. **Acknowledge your emotional pain.** Turn toward your experience with kindness.

2. **Be understanding with yourself and your situation.** You don't have to know exactly why you are feeling discomfort, but you can offer yourself context and realistic evidence that you are face-to-face with a challenging moment. Try offering yourself one of your chosen compassionate coaching mantras.

3. **Be mindful.** Without judgment, remind your parent brain that you are struggling in *this moment*. Refrain from rehashing past mistakes or worrying about future problems.

4. **Normalize your struggle.** This doesn't deny that it is painful. It reminds you that you're not alone and this is an expected part of the parent (and human) experience.

5. **Choose to be effective.** If there is a problem to be solved, think through solutions. Sometimes there is no solution, and sometimes there is no actual problem (just your amygdala setting off false alarms). Notice which is true for you, and act accordingly.

Here is an example from Diego:

1. Ugh. Not knowing what my kid wants is tough. I know he will eventually settle down—it's just so uncomfortable not knowing.

2. Of course it's tough—I'm now responsible for keeping this little guy alive! And obviously he can't tell me what he needs, so it's a guessing game. Nobody is perfect. All I can do is continue to try to do the next right thing.

3. Deep breath. This part doesn't last forever; he always eventually settles down.

4. I know that it's not just me. My wife, Mark—it's hard for them too.

5. Okay, I need some extra help. Maybe I'll ask my sister to help us out and see if she has tips on this parenting thing.

In your Training Journal, write down a parenting challenge from this week. Use these steps to formulate your own self-compassionate response. For the next week, aim to complete this exercise for at least three different parenting challenges that arise.

Your Parent Brain as an Effective Problem Solver

A helpful way to get your parent brain unstuck from shame-and-blame thinking is to switch gears and engage in some PFC-initiated problem solving with a challenging situation. If you face realistic, solvable problems—great, go for it! See these problems as chances to learn to navigate new or stressful challenges. Sometimes effective problem solving will lead your parent brain to realize that you haven't actually made a mistake and that you can accept this uncomfortable challenge. Rewiring your parent brain to more readily activate problem-solving mode instead of self-critical mode requires insight, perspective shifting, and cognitive flexibility—all initiated in your PFC. This part of your brain can engage in effective problem solving when you tune in to your current situation with openness and curiosity, instead of your usual shame-and-blame story. Your PFC helps you take a step back to see your challenge from a different perspective and explore new and innovative ways to move past the problem at hand.

For example:

Mark noticed himself worrying about how often his infant was fussing and crying. He was trying everything he could to keep her healthy and happy, but her constant fussing led him to worry about her well-being and whether he was taking proper care of her. When Mark noticed himself becoming anxious each time she fussed, he decided to search for an effective solution. Mark chose to call his baby's pediatrician to schedule a checkup. After all, he was a new parent and certainly didn't have all of the answers. Mark's decision to seek an effective solution allowed him to break free from the guilt of self-blame and the discomfort of his anxiety.

Diego found himself in a similar situation, feeling panicked and afraid each time his baby began to cry. Despite his efforts to soothe him, Diego was sure he had the fussiest baby on the block and felt nervous and ashamed each time he began to fuss. When Diego tried to shift gears into effective problem-solving mode and look for a solution, he remembered that at his son's most recent checkup, the doctor told him his baby had colic. The doctor had assured him that he was perfectly healthy, and colic is actually quite common. Recalling this, Diego realized that there was no real problem solving to be done in this situation. Although his distress at hearing his baby's cries was uncomfortable, Diego knew he could tolerate it and recognize that his son's fussing was not a reason to feel shame or fear.

When Diego and Mark decided to shift gears into effective problem-solving mode, they were able to move forward with similar challenges in different ways, based on their individual circumstances.

Research has found that when we engage in open, flexible thinking, the different areas of the brain are better able to communicate with each other, resulting in effective problem solving *and* decreased anxiety overall. If decreased anxiety isn't enough of a reason to problem solve rather than self-blame, know that researchers have also found that the brain actually receives a pleasurable reward signal when it effectively problem solves (Oh et al., 2020). This reward signal is related to the same area of your brain associated with pleasurable experiences like food, socializing with friends or loved ones, and orgasms. Problem solving can actually be a rewarding and pleasurable experience, similar to completing a puzzle, discovering a new favorite restaurant, or listening to your favorite true-crime podcast.

Parent Brain Rewiring Exercise: Finding Your Effective Parent Brain Response

Think of a parenting challenge you encountered in the past few weeks. You will explore the three approaches your parent brain can follow in response to this challenge. Using the Shame and Blame versus Problem Solving Worksheet, take note of your thoughts, feelings, and behaviors. After thinking through each response, rate your anxiety level (0 to 10, lowest to highest). Recall that Mark's anxiety never disappeared, but at lower levels he could make room for the other emotions that arose with his actions.

You can download a PDF of the Shame and Blame versus Problem Solving Worksheet and see Mark's example at www.newharbinger.com/50300.

How Self-Compassion Exercises Rewire Your Parent Brain for Less Stress and Anxiety

When parenthood serves up a difficult moment, whether your newborn won't stop crying or your teenager is struggling in school, you can choose to disengage from shame-and-blame thinking and instead activate your PFC to do its important job of planning and problem solving. And without all that shame and blame taking up your precious mental space, you can more effectively navigate any and all challenging situations you encounter.

There may be times, as you move through this training program, that your parent brain reverts back to shame-and-blame mode. When you feel self-criticism creeping in, remind yourself that beating yourself up will only keep you stuck and that true freedom from stress and anxiety comes with acceptance and self-compassion. By rewiring your parent brain to be less critical and more self-compassionate, you will free up your PFC to help you live the life you really want.

CHAPTER 3

Choosing Reality over Catastrophe

Catastrophic thinking can become a reflex for any anxious parent, as illustrated by the story of Sarah and Beth.

Sarah and Beth were sisters-in-law—and best friends. Over the years, they shared many parenting thrills and spills and supported each other through it all. Of course, they were two different people with different life experiences, temperaments, and parenting practices. They each felt blessed to have the other in their life for guidance, support, and sometimes a shoulder to cry on.

Sarah and Beth would compare notes on the challenges of parenting preteen girls: Sarah's twelve-year-old, Zoe, and Beth's eleven-year-old, Charlotte. In one of their weekly chats, they discussed their daughters' recent shifts in friend groups. Sarah noted how Zoe was struggling with "girl drama" as the girls she had always been close with seemed to be moving at a faster pace, using technology and social media in ways Sarah was not comfortable with and starting to leave Zoe out of their group chats and get-togethers.

Beth empathized, as Charlotte was experiencing similar social upheaval. Charlotte had always been a sporty girl and enjoyed hanging out with the boys just as much as with her girl friends. Charlotte's comfort socializing with both boys and girls, and her desire to kick a soccer ball around or have an impromptu Nerf war during a playdate, had never been a problem with her girl friends before. But since starting sixth grade, her social world was shifting; what was acceptable in fifth grade was now leaving Charlotte feeling left out and excluded.

Sarah's Parent Brain Default State: Catastrophic Thinking

Sarah was spending more time thinking about Zoe's social challenges. These thoughts were in her mind when she awoke, dogged her throughout her day, and kept her awake at night. She could not seem to escape her worries about Zoe's friendship troubles. Her distress grew, as she could not seem to find a solution to the situation. Sarah's mind was constantly reviewing all the negative potential for Zoe. She imagined her daughter experiencing a lifetime of social isolation, feeling like an outsider, and low self-esteem. She worried that Zoe would seek a new friend group and begin to connect with "the wrong kind of kids." Sarah's constant worry thoughts kept spiraling out of control: What if she begins hanging out with the kids in her grade who have more problems, because at least they will accept her? What if she starts using drugs or cutting or develops an eating disorder? What if she feels so lonely, isolated, and rejected that she tries to take her own life someday?

Beth's Parent Brain Default State: Realistic Thinking

Beth was spending more time worrying about Charlotte's social life and friend group transitions. One day, after wasting countless hours googling topics such as "signs your child is struggling socially" and "help for tween girl friendship drama," Beth was able to take a step back from her fears. She realized this preoccupation not only offered zero value to Charlotte but was also hurting Beth's own mental health and overall well-being. Beth had gotten stuck in a thinking trap, believing that if only she could think her way through Charlotte's challenges, she could prevent her from experiencing pain and suffering. She could no longer separate what her daughter was truly experiencing and feeling from her own interpretation of the situation. Beth decided it was time to reboot her approach.

Beth knew she needed to take a step back to get a more objective perspective, to determine whether this was normal adolescent growing pains or a real problem requiring an intervention. Beth decided to keep a log of her worries about Charlotte's social life. Whenever she found herself stuck in a worry thought, she would write it down, then practice forcing herself to "change the channel" in her mind, as if clicking a remote away from her worries and on to a more grounded, productive thinking channel. Next, Beth decided to review her daily list of worries at a set time every day. During this time, Beth would view the list objectively rather than emotionally. At 8 p.m. each day, when the kids were absorbed in a TV show and the house was a little quieter, Beth would review her list and assess how accurate each worry thought was. For any inaccurate thoughts, she challenged herself to jot down a more realistic interpretation of the challenge at hand.

Beth practiced holding this daily "worry time" for the next week. Soon she could observe her extreme worries rather than getting sucked into their spiral. The more she practiced observing them objectively, the more easily she could redirect her attention to the current moment. By systematically noticing and then assessing the accuracy of her worried thoughts, she was able to take some of the wind out of their sails. As the days passed, she still felt a sting of distress when a thought such as Charlotte is going to be friendless forever showed up. Despite the momentary gut punch, Beth began finding it easier to choose how to respond to her worry thoughts, instead of being overwhelmed by the painful feelings they triggered. This work was not easy for Beth, but the payoff was significant. Less time wasted thinking about how to rescue Charlotte meant more time to actually spend with her daughter, fostering a close bond and modeling how to live a meaningful life of connection.

From Catastrophic to Realistic Thinking

Being a parent entails inevitably witnessing your child experience a variety of life challenges, with a dash of everyday pain and suffering. Your parent brain's default reaction to these moments is to offer up a plethora of worry thoughts and images, highlighting all the ways your child's well-being and happiness are at risk and all of the dangers that may await them. The good news is that there is another path forward. You can't stop your brain from experiencing a cacophony of catastrophic cognitions (given its hardwired orders to protect your child at all costs), but you can change how you react to them. In doing so, you will no longer be held captive by your worry thoughts but instead can choose how and when to respond to them.

This chapter will help you learn to:

- Notice when you are engaged in an unhelpful catastrophic thinking cycle

- Disengage from catastrophic worry thoughts and more efficiently bring your attention back to the present moment

- Enhance your ability to evaluate life scenarios through a logical versus emotionally reactive lens

- Distinguish between a true problem to solve and general life uncertainty to tolerate

When Danger Detection Leads to Ineffective Worry Mode

As we've discussed, your brain's ability to recognize when you're facing a potential threat and encourage you to seek safety is critical for survival. You can't live without this brain function. But you *can* live without the worry loop of unhelpful, catastrophic thinking. When your parent brain points out a potential threat, it can either shift to problem-solving mode or get stuck in a worry loop. Although Beth and Sarah found themselves in similar situations, their responses to their daughters' social challenges were distinctly different.

Both Beth and Sarah were witnessing their daughters' concerning social interactions. Beth was on carpool duty; driving a few of Charlotte's neighborhood friends home from school, she overheard an awkward conversation. Charlotte invited the girls over to play backyard soccer. The girls all had different excuses for not being able to come over, but it seemed clear they would rather get their braces tightened than play soccer with Charlotte. Similarly, Sarah had witnessed her daughter being dismissed by the girls she used to be closest with at school. Sarah volunteered at Zoe's school cafeteria once a month, and during her most recent shift she noticed Zoe sitting at the end of the lunch table, attempting to join a conversation with peers and consistently being overpowered by louder girls who seemed to dominate.

Beth's brain observed Charlotte's social challenge and sent her the amygdala-driven signal: *Danger! Charlotte is entering new friendship terrain, and her old friends may not value her company like they used to. This could lead to pain and suffering.* Beth's brain then shifted from threat-detection mode to problem-solving mode, to consider potential solutions and mitigate risk. After thinking things over for a bit, Beth decided on an action plan. Given the events she had observed in the carpool, she decided to chat with Charlotte over an after-school snack about how Charlotte felt during that situation. She was prepared to encourage Charlotte to connect with peers who share her interest in sports and help her brainstorm ways to connect with kids whose interests align more closely with hers. Beth knew it was important to hear how Charlotte felt in the situation (rather than jumping to conclusions based on her parent brain's interpretations alone), and she was prepared to offer to support Charlotte however she could. Operating in problem-solving mode instead of catastrophic-thinking mode gave both Beth and Charlotte a sense of relief, knowing this was not the end of the world and there were reasonable next steps to be taken.

When Sarah observed Zoe's social challenge, her brain also sent her a similar amygdala-driven signal. From there, instead of shifting into problem-solving mode, Sarah found herself trapped in an ever-expanding web of potential hardships Zoe might experience due to her soft-spoken nature. Her brain posed unanswerable questions, such as *What if this is just the start of never being able to speak up in a conversation? What if she gives up trying to be heard and accepted and believes she's unworthy of friendship? What if she never truly connects with anyone again and is isolated and alone forever?* Sarah's amygdala-driven threat signal initiated a chain of thoughts that spiraled toward catastrophe until she felt completely overwhelmed. Once her daughter's problems felt that big, it was no longer possible to engage in practical problem solving. Before she knew what hit her, Sarah had shifted from worrying about Zoe being crowded out of the conversation to fearing Zoe would live a life of isolation and misery.

As soon as your parent brain detects a potential threat, you'll find yourself at a fork in the road. Your parent brain can select path A and circle round and round the initial threat, building upon worry thoughts and "what ifs" until the situation feels insurmountable. Or it can select path B and shift from threat-detection to problem-solving mode. If you've found yourself taking path A more than you'd like to admit, you're in good company (most parents can relate!). The exercises in this chapter will help you venture down path B instead.

The Function of Catastrophic Worry Thoughts

Before we help you more efficiently move past catastrophic worry thoughts, let's understand the function of these uncomfortable thoughts. Why do you think your parent brain is constantly pointing out all the awful things that could occur and all the ways life could go off track for you and your loved ones? Which of these answers comes to mind?

1. My parent brain loves torturing me.

2. My parent brain is trying to help me.

Believe it or not, the correct answer is not A. Your parent brain is *not* trying to torture you with those catastrophic thoughts and images—although it can feel that way. Your advanced reasoning skills have probably deduced that therefore the answer must be B: your parent brain is trying to help you.

Catastrophic worry thoughts aim to startle you with the worst dangers imaginable, hoping that awareness of these lurking threats will protect you and/or your loved ones from harm. Worry thoughts are mental worker bees, buzzing about, pointing out potential obstacles.

Your Parent Brain in Catastrophic Thinking Mode

Generating catastrophic worry thoughts is your parent brain's way of prompting you to plan for an uncertain future and take corrective action when appropriate. Even if there were a way you could completely eradicate catastrophic worry thoughts (there isn't), you would be ill advised to flip the Off switch and eliminate your brain's ability to produce them. Catastrophic worry thoughts can be extremely helpful

---

and necessary for survival. When there is true danger or a harmful threat ahead, you need your amygdala to sound the alarm to keep you safe. Imagine you are driving your family on a road trip, notice your eyes getting heavy, and feel yourself getting increasingly more drowsy. Your parent brain may send you this useful prompt: *What if I fall asleep at the wheel and the car veers into another lane or into the median of the highway or off a bridge?* If your overactive amygdala takes hold, you may be consumed in your own mental worst nightmare, as your catastrophizing thoughts and images escalate into overwhelming anxiety that renders you ineffective. However, if, after this startling message from your amygdala, you observe the reality of your situation rather than going along with the worst-case scenario, your PFC can help you choose a new course of action. You then might problem solve to hand off the driving or find a rest area, or better yet, a hotel where your family can stay the night. It's important for your parent brain to be able to send out danger messages when needed, prompting you to choose a safer, healthier alternative. It can be uncomfortable to receive your brain's danger messaging, but that mental zap is important to keep you in check and encourage you to make healthy, safe decisions.

Let's see just how quickly catastrophic thinking can take over and push aside important tasks.

> At work one day, Sarah sees an article about how teenage girls require social connections to thrive. She tries to put her fears aside and focus on the presentation she is working on, but she keeps worrying more and more about Zoe's social challenges. She tries to multitask, mentally reviewing all of Zoe's social mishaps to date, while continuing her preparation. It is impossible for her PFC to effectively review both Zoe's social well-being and her important presentation simultaneously. Since Sarah has bought into the catastrophic worry thoughts about Zoe's social challenges, it's only natural for her parent brain to prioritize worrying about her daughter's well-being over her employer's presentation.

The Cost of Getting Stuck in Catastrophic Thinking Mode

It's not just uncomfortable to be stuck in catastrophic worry mode; it's also inefficient. Imagine the energy a boxer needs to win a fight. Once the match is over, how much energy do you think the boxer has left to accomplish other life tasks that day? By definition, when you use your energy to review every possible threat to you or your family, you'll have little left to do much else. When your parent brain is stuck in a worry loop, it consumes excessive energy. As your brain becomes more reactive to potential threats, it directs your attention to unhelpful or irrelevant issues instead of focusing on the important task at hand.

Even worse, although catastrophic worry thoughts offer up important information, they can also inflict painful, emotionally evocative content with little to no practical value. For example, one afternoon Sarah was driving to pick Zoe up at school when a news announcer began reporting on the rising rates of suicide among teenagers. Sarah was riveted. She began to sweat and feel lightheaded. At the school, when Zoe hopped into the back seat, Sarah was silent. Her parent brain was racing with thoughts such as *What if this is how it ends for Zoe? What if she cannot live with the painful feeling of rejection and takes her own life? How could I possibly go on?* Sarah's spiraling thoughts had put up an invisible barrier between her and her daughter as she drove silently, feeling terrified and out of control. At that moment, the only things Sarah actually needed to attend to were the road ahead and her daughter in the back seat. The time she spent with her catastrophic thinking could have been spent in conversation, starting with "How was school?" Though there was no immediate danger, Sarah's anxious parent brain pulled her away from a precious opportunity to connect with her child.

Catastrophic Thinking for Two

Catastrophic thinking about your child and their challenges not only negatively impacts you as the parent, but it can also negatively affect your child's experience of exactly how big an issue they are facing. Research indicates that catastrophizing about a child's pain is significantly correlated with the amount of perceived pain and functional impairment the child will experience (Guite et al., 2011). For example, if you find out at your child's dental exam that they need to have their wisdom teeth pulled and you react with fear and concern, your child's mirror neurons will actually mimic your emotional state of fear and concern. Instead of reacting fearfully, take this as an opportunity to meet the unpleasant news with a deep breath and a nod of confidence toward your child, reminding them this is a necessary experience they can handle.

By directly addressing your tendency to engage in catastrophic thinking about your child's potential pain and suffering, you will send a more adaptive signal to your child, communicating that even when life is difficult, they are competent and resilient and can handle all that life throws their way. In addition to improving your child's functioning, you will feel better and experience less psychological pain yourself. Remember, if worrying about your child's potential pain could help prevent or even reduce their future suffering and increase their life satisfaction, we would absolutely encourage you to do so (and in fact, we authors would do the same). Unfortunately, that is just now how it works. As the research suggests, buying into your catastrophic worry thoughts is much more likely to exacerbate your child's experience of emotional pain and decrease their ability to believe in their coping abilities and resilience (Guite et al., 2011). Rewiring your parent brain to more readily engage in realistic thinking instead of catastrophic thinking will benefit both you and your child.

Brain Spam Parading as Priority Mail

At every waking moment your brain is sorting through a plethora of inputs to help you simultaneously manage that moment and maximize your odds of long-term survival. Your brain constantly scans your internal environment to determine whether all bodily systems are performing effectively and scans your external environment for risks and opportunities. It also continuously reviews your key learnings and memories to pull out critical information that may help you meet your present and future goals. This is a whole lot of information to have buzzing around in your mind. Luckily, your PFC's data sorting capabilities can help with reviewing and prioritizing all this data. Yet it may still misidentify catastrophic worry thoughts as helpful information when they are actually "brain spam" (BS), much like the spam messages in your email inbox. But you can enhance your brain's information sorting capabilities through the exercises outlined in this chapter.

Parent Brain Rewiring Exercise: Helpful Information or Brain Spam?

Take a moment to visualize your email inbox. How likely are you to open an email titled "You Just Won a FREE Trip to Jamaica! CLICK NOW TO REDEEM" versus an email titled "Your Monthly Utility Bill"? Some emails are obviously spam; others contain helpful information (HI). Of course, it is also possible to receive messages that aren't so black-and-white and require some further investigation. By engaging in the following logic-based exercise, you'll be better able to sort through catastrophic worry thoughts, place most in your mental trash folder, and avoid wasting time and energy reviewing their irrelevant content that you could better devote to more deserving aspects of your life.

For the next week, keep a log in your Training Journal of all the moments when you find yourself experiencing a worry thought. You can see an example Worry Thought Tracking Log based on Sarah's experience and a blank downloadable PDF at www.newharbinger.com/50300.

Write down:

- Date/Time

- Details of the situation: where you were, what you were doing

- The content of your worry thought

- Whether your parent brain offered you helpful information (write *HI*) or brain spam (write *BS*)

After one week, take some time to reflect:

- Draw a pie chart of BS versus HI to help show your parent brain just how frequently catastrophic worry thoughts are actually BS. What percentage of your catastrophic worry thoughts from the past week turned out to provide you with HI and what percentage were actually BS?

Parent Brain Rewiring Exercise: How Do You React to Your Catastrophic Worry Thoughts?

Over the next week, practice noting when you are feeling stressed, anxious, or worried and write down the thoughts that surface. To track key data from these trigger moments, use your Training Journal or download the CW Thought Tracking Log (and a completed sample from Sarah's experience) at www.new harbinger.com/50300.

Write down:

- Date/Time

- Details of the situation: where you were, what you were doing

- The content of your worry

- Whether your parent brain entered problem-solving mode (write *PS*) or catastrophic worry mode (write *CW*)

After one week, take some time to reflect:

- Over the course of the last week, upon encountering a worry thought, did you enter a CW thinking loop or PS mode?

- As you became a more objective observer of how you react to your worry thoughts, did you notice any shifts in terms of spending less time in CW mode and more in effective PS mode?

The first step in rewiring your parent brain to spend less time stuck in catastrophic worry mode is to become a skilled observer of this phenomenon. You cannot break free of a thinking style if you are unaware of when you are engaging in it. By paying attention to your mental chatter, you'll be able to more rapidly discern the difference between a thought that delivers CW information and a thought that delivers HI. This will help strengthen your ability to shift from CW mode to effective PS mode.

Time to Challenge Your Brain Spam

The brain rewiring exercises in the following section will enhance your mind's ability to experience a CW thought with the calm stance of a scientist observing a specimen under a microscope instead of the terror-filled lens of a homeowner observing an intruder smashing in a window in the middle of the night. By learning to apply a rational lens to a CW thought, you will be better able to see it for what it is—and what it is not. You can see all that brain spam info as neither helpful nor true. By training your brain to better observe helpful information, rather than buy into the brain spam courtesy of your CW thoughts, you are rewiring your parent brain to more efficiently move past these thoughts instead of feeling stuck in them.

Parent Brain Rewiring Exercise: From Catastrophic Worry to Realistic Thinking

For the next week, write down every CW that surfaces. Compare the evidence to support the CW thought's predictions with the evidence against the CW thought's predictions. Notice any changes in your distress level after applying a realistic lens to your CW thoughts.

To track key data from these "trigger moments," use your Training Journal or download the CW Thought Challenging Log and a completed sample from Beth's experience at www.newharbinger.com/50300.

Write down:

- Date/Time

- CW thought

- Level of emotional distress (0–10): pre-challenging

- Evidence to support CW thought

- Evidence to dispute CW thought

- Level of emotional distress (0–10): post-challenging

After one week, take some time to reflect:

- Was it difficult to challenge your CW thoughts? How quickly did you come up with evidence for and against your worries?

- Did you notice any changes to your thoughts—thinking more or less about the CW thoughts after this exercise? Or were you able to freely move on to the more important things in your day?

Catastrophic Worry Thoughts Leading to a Core Fear

Each new CW thought may at first appear unique, but as you strengthen your PFC's ability to observe and assess these thoughts, you will realize your worry thoughts all lead to your core fear. We describe this to clients as the same core fear showing up under the guise of an array of CW thoughts, similar to the same person wearing many different scary Halloween costumes.

Parent Brain Rewiring Exercise: Downward Arrow to Your Core Parent Fears

You are taking an important step: by identifying and contacting your core fears rather than trying to hide from them (which only gives them more power over you), you're empowering yourself to more effectively manage them. The more targeted work you do to move through and past these fears, the easier it will be to disentangle yourself from all the different-seeming CW thoughts that are just variations on a theme. No need to rewire your brain to manage each variation. To prove it, follow these steps in your Training Journal (referring to Sarah's example, which follows):

1. Pick any CW thought you noted in the previous exercise and write it down.

2. Draw a downward arrow and ask yourself, *If that feared event were to come true, then what would be so bad about that?* Write your answer.

3. Draw another arrow and ask yourself the same question.

4. Repeat step 2 until you recognize that you have made contact with your core fear.

5. Look back at the previous CW thoughts you tracked. For each worry thought, consider whether it's in any way connected to your core fear. For each thought that does, write CF.

6. What percentage of your worry thoughts connect in some way to your core fear?

Here is how Sarah completed this exercise:

Zoe rejected by friends.

Zoe grows depressed.

Zoe spends increasing time alone.

Zoe begins cutting and using drugs.

Zoe tries to kill herself.

Zoe gets hospitalized and we try all kinds of treatments and nothing works and Zoe lives a lifetime of misery, barely hanging on and wishing she were not alive.

All I can do is witness her experiencing pain and suffering, and there is nothing I can do to help her.

I WILL BE TORTURED BY LIVING IN ENDLESS EMOTIONAL PAIN, AS I MUST IDLY STAND BY AND WATCH ZOE SUFFERING.

On completing this exercise, Sarah was shocked. She'd had no idea that what underlay all her fears about Zoe's potential emotional suffering was actually fear of her own emotional suffering as Zoe's mother. She knew she found nothing more distressing than seeing her children's well-being threatened, but she didn't realize that all her fears about her children's life difficulties stemmed from her own core fear of experiencing excruciating emotional pain, with no way to escape the horror.

The Flip Side of Your Catastrophic Worry Thoughts: Your Values

The content of a CW thought highlights the aspects of your life that you value most and therefore are most concerned about protecting. Generating CW thoughts requires so much energy that your brain wouldn't waste time creating them on topics of little importance. You will never encounter BS such as *What if I spill this bottle of water?* It's worth taking time to allow your BS thoughts to shine light on what you value most in your life. As you continue rewiring your parent brain, you will find that you are more able to engage in those valued aspects of your life.

Parent Brain Rewiring Exercise: Values Underlying Your Catastrophic Worry Thoughts

Sarah's core fear of her own emotional suffering was deeply linked to her value of being the best possible mother. But if she was stuck in emotional suffering, how could she effectively navigate the life she wanted for herself and her kids?

Here are more examples of the connection between Sarah's worries and her core values:

1. *Zoe seems like she's not in the mood to chat about her day. Is this what the beginning of self-isolation looks like?*

   Values social connections and parent-child relationship

2. *What if Zoe left the oven on after cooking lunch? I should have been watching her the whole time to make sure.*

Values safety of loved ones

3. *Am I forgetting something important I have to do today?*

   Values efficiency so there is more time to spend at home with the family later

For the thought sequence you created in the previous exercise, create a new column where you write down the core value and critical aspect of your life that this thought is ineffectively attempting to protect.

How Thought-Challenging Exercises Rewire Your Parent Brain to Reduce Stress and Anxiety

Catastrophic thinking increases stress and anxiety. When your PFC sends catastrophic thinking messages to your amygdala, it reacts fearfully. Wired to detect danger, it senses this in your catastrophic thoughts and releases stress hormones, initiating the fight-flight-freeze response. While this response is essential when you're in actual danger, when triggered by catastrophizing it creates highly uncomfortable and unhelpful anxiety and panic. When your PFC offers a more realistic, balanced assessment of the situation at hand, you don't trigger your amygdala to initiate the fight-flight-freeze response. This allows you to react less based in fear and more grounded in realistic thinking, without anxiety and panic hampering your efforts to tackle the situation.

As you engage in the brain rewiring exercises in this chapter, you're giving your parent brain an upgraded CW thought spam filter. You're sparing your amygdala and hypothalamus the rush of catastrophic worries, so there's no need to signal your body to prepare for true danger. And although you still might get the initial jolting false alarm of worry, you will now have easier access to your newly strengthened realistic thinking skills courtesy of your PFC. Your hippocampus will store these memories of new encounters with realistic thinking to help you with future false alarms. By rewiring your parent brain to operate with greater information sorting capabilities, you can more effectively and efficiently distinguish truly critical information to be considered from attention-grabbing but irrelevant spam.

CHAPTER 4

The Gift of Your Presence

We begin this chapter with the stories of Jenny and Melody, friends and mothers.

Jenny kept waking up with the self-chiding thought, Today is the day you must be a better mom. *Between busy work demands, her two children's increasingly complex activities schedule, and her attempts to weave in a tiny bit of self-care, it seemed she had no time to actually connect with and be emotionally available to her children. Right then, Jenny made the decision to prioritize spending at least one hour a week with each of them. She asked her ten-year-old, Ava, and her twelve-year-old, Ben, to each choose an activity they would enjoy (or at least not find excruciatingly annoying) to do with her. She told them she would reserve this special time just for them and prioritize their hour together the same way she would any other meeting or event she committed to.*

Both Ben and Ava took a few days to think about what they wanted to do with their weekly "Mom and me" time. With some discussion and negotiation, it was decided that Jenny would play Ava's favorite board games with her and cook new recipes with Ben, a budding foodie. Jenny tried to show equal excitement about both of these plans, but she was much more excited about spending an hour a week on culinary adventures and much less excited about the boredom of board games. Not that she enjoyed her son any more than her daughter; Jenny and Ava had a very close bond. But Jenny hated playing board games and dreaded spending quality time this way. However, as the "good mom" she always strived to be, she'd made sure the home was well stocked with board games, and she reminded herself that family game nights could be a healthy alternative to otherwise endless screen time. So Jenny committed herself to this special time with Ava, determined to share her delight in moving little figurines across the board.

When the first "Mom and me" time came around, Ava selected Monopoly. Jenny felt subtle but palpable feelings of dread. *Does Monopoly ever end? How can I fake some believable interest in this painfully boring game?* She comforted herself that she'd committed to only one hour. As Ava started laying out the game and reviewing the instructions, Jenny began to think through the emails she needed to get to after the kids went to bed. For the remainder of the hour, she was 5 percent engaged in Monopoly and 95 percent mentally flipping through to-do lists. As she moved her piece across the board while thinking through the week's dinner recipes, she felt a sting of guilt for being such a distracted disappointment of a mom.

Jenny told her neighbor, Melody, about this new goal of spending more quality time with her kids. Melody thought this was a wonderful idea, and she proposed the same plan to her children, Aiden and Sydney. Aiden, who had a growing interest in graphic novels and illustration, chose to take an art class together at the local community college. Sydney decided to spend the time kicking a soccer ball around at the local park. Melody was never much of an athlete and couldn't quite understand what made sports so enjoyable to so many people. But, similar to Jenny, she was dedicated to honoring her commitment to quality time with her children. On the morning of Sydney's first "Mom and me" day, Melody checked the weather and noticed it was going to be chilly and rainy. Her brain was quick to point out the misery she had in store, offering up thoughts like It's going to be wet and freezing out there and There's no chance you'll actually enjoy this hour. Luckily, Melody had been working on enhancing her mindfulness abilities over the past year or so. Using mindfulness, she was able to notice these thoughts as they arose and gently bring herself back to the current moment. Although Melody's brain seemed determined to point out just how unpleasant kicking a ball around on a rainy, chilly day was going to be, she was able to keep anchoring herself back to the present moment. Each time an unpleasant thought about the upcoming activity arose in her mind, she simply noticed the thought and shifted her focus to what truly mattered most to her—investing time and energy in meaningful connection with her daughter.

Jenny's Parent Brain Default State: Mindless and Disengaged from the Present

Unlike Melody, Jenny hasn't learned how to apply the art and science of mindfulness to parenting. Jenny has an overactive "monkey mind" swinging from one thought to the next, constantly seeking out something shiny and interesting to grab on to. Jenny lets her mind call the shots and pull her this way and that, deciding what to attend to and when, rather than guiding it to follow her lead and attending to what is most important to her. She takes all of her thoughts seriously and believes all are worthy of reviewing and, at times, wrestling with. When Jenny's monkey mind takes over, it pulls her out of the present moment and takes away from treasured times with her family. She'll review grocery lists and carpool schedules in her mind rather than being in the present moment with her kids. Jenny could benefit from learning to engage her brain's mindfulness muscles to engage with necessary thoughts and disengage from unimportant ones, allowing her to be truly present with her family. By rewiring her parent brain to be more mindful, Jenny can deepen her ability to live more fully in the present moment rather than being pulled out of it by her mind's endless thoughts.

Melody's Parent Brain Default State: Mindful and Engaged in the Present

Melody's monkey mind is also eager to play, swinging from thought to thought. Similar to Jenny's, Melody's mind also offers unhelpful thoughts trying to pull her out of the present moment and sabotage quality family time. All the mindfulness training in the world can't prevent the human mind from babbling on about anything and everything it finds noteworthy. But just because Melody's mind (and your mind too) may choose to share its running dialogue does not mean that Melody (or you) needs to attend to it.

Thanks to Melody's ongoing efforts to enhance her mental mindfulness muscles, she has a strong ability to notice the presence of her thoughts without being pulled out of the present moment. She can choose to either attend to a thought or feeling or guide her attention back to the current moment. While Jenny's mental chatter left her largely disengaged and distracted from Monopoly with her daughter, Melody was able to stay present and make the most of a damp, chilly soccer game with her daughter. By continuing to work her mindfulness muscles each day, Melody will find it increasingly easier to guide her mind toward satisfaction and meaning in her family life, rather than being caught up in the endless thought stream that her parent brain can never truly shut off. You can do the same.

From Mindless to Mindful Living

As parents, it's absolutely essential for us to be able to stay grounded in the present. When we aren't present, we find ourselves feeling reactive, disorganized, distractible, and disengaged from what matters most. As life's precious moments fly by, you deserve to be truly present with your child, savoring time together and creating lasting memories, instead of feeling bogged down by stress and anxious thoughts. Mindful parenting is about intentionally practicing being here and now with your child and family. Think of mindfulness as *attention with intention*. When modern family life brings endless multitasking and distractions, mindfulness is your go-to tool to bring your attention back to essential things. Think about how much more you would appreciate one hour of truly connecting with your family than ten hours of distracted, multitasking time together. And you don't need extra hours in the day to make mindfulness a key component of your life—you can mindfully go for a walk, have a conversation, eat a meal, or even play a board game. No need to wait for the kids to be older or the to-do list to be shorter—today is a perfect day to be a more mindful parent. It is time to embrace the moment, no matter what the moment holds.

This chapter will help you learn to:

- Gain a practical understanding of mindfulness and mindful parenting practices

- Attend to and connect with your child

- Slow down so you can *choose* how to respond to stressful situations rather than responding emotionally or impulsively

- Listen to your child and hear what they are expressing rather than your mind's interpretation of it

- Enhance your mind's ability to recognize mental noise rather than get caught up in it

- Disengage from BS and reengage in the present moment

- Spend more time connecting with your child rather than worrying about them

Mindful Living for Two

Practicing mindfulness offers a myriad of benefits not only for you as an individual but also for your child and family. Parents often wish their children would be more mindful—to put the electronics down and be more present with the family, or be more mindful of their manners at the dinner table. Remember that teaching your child to be more mindful cannot be outsourced; the best way is to practice mindfulness yourself.

Mindful parenting means doing what it takes to slow down, stop the multitasking, and be present with your child and family. When you are truly present in the moment, you are cultivating a meaningful connection with your child and creating treasured memories together. As you take intentional steps to mindfully attend to the moment with your family (think: *attention with intention*), you model this behavior for your child. By observing your actions, your child will learn how to be curious, be present, take their time, and enjoy all that life has to offer. As children grow, many parents wish they could slow down time. While we can't stop the clock, parents and children alike can learn to put down the distractions and be together in the moment, savoring whatever it brings.

Your Parent Brain in Mindless Living Mode

Mindlessness isn't all bad. Mindless living is not only natural, but it is also adaptive. If we were always mindfully attending to the current moment, we humans would get nothing done. We would be so busy taking in all of the sensations and nuances of our current experience that we would not have the spare brain power to discover fire or invent the wheel or problem solve to allow for progress and advancement. Thanks to the useful tool of mindlessness, you can multitask. You can walk and chew gum. You can drive a car while listening to a podcast. You can feed your baby a bottle while listening to the riveting story your other little one has to share about her snack-time adventures at preschool that day.

Just as every home should be stocked with a toolbox filled with tools, so should your mind. Your brain is equipped with both mindless and mindful capabilities, offering you multiple modes of operating. This allows for mindless moments, mindful moments, and an array of moments in between. However, there is a time and place to use any tool, and even a useful tool can shift from being helpful to harmful. When you have a picture to hang or any nail needing a solid bang, there is no better option than a hammer. But if you destructively hammer away at drywall with no clear purpose, that helpful hammer becomes harmful. The same analogy holds true for mindlessness. If you are always multitasking, problem solving, or mentally thinking through past or future concerns, you will never experience the richness and pleasure of your life. You will never truly taste your food, appreciate awe-inspiring sunsets, or hear the exquisite sound of your child's giggle. With this understanding, it's time to rediscover and enhance your mindfulness abilities, so you can experience more moments of true engagement, connection, and joy with yourself and your family.

Your Brain on Mindfulness

There is so much hype about the benefits of mindfulness in the popular press and on social media these days that before we formally introduce mindfulness to our clients, we first try to elicit their current understanding of it. Often we hear clients equate mindfulness to a form of relaxation training or sometimes even a breathing practice. Mindfulness training is actually hard work; it is not always relaxing. Gaining the ability to notice the urge to get sucked into a thought or feeling and then actively guide your attention back to the present moment takes effort and intention.

So what exactly is mindfulness, and why bother attempting to rewire your brain to be more mindful? Mindfulness can be defined as a nonjudgmental focus on your present experience. Notice: nothing about turning off your thoughts, blocking negative ones, or not getting distracted. Mindfulness means noticing the full range of your present experience, without negatively reacting to or trying to change it. It means intentionally bringing your attention to your current experience—and keeping it there. When you work your mindfulness muscles, as you'll soon learn, you may be shocked to see all the places your mind goes, bouncing here, there, and all over. Again, the goal is never to block or turn off your thoughts but simply to notice them, as Melody did, and then return to the present moment, again and again. Through this practice, you may find yourself becoming less stressed and irritable, and a more connected and joyful parent.

Fortunately, your brain's ability to mindfully attend to the present moment is not something you are born with or without, such as blue eyes or brown hair. We can develop and enhance our mindfulness capabilities with practice and intention. Thanks to neuroimaging studies, we know that regularly hitting the "mindfulness brain gym" is associated with positive changes to brain structures and neurocircuitry. For example, recent research demonstrates that ongoing mindfulness training can enhance brain functioning (Wheeler et al., 2017), including decreased activation of the amygdala, increased hippocampus size, and even decreased brain aging overall. A more mindful brain is associated with decreased emotional reactivity, enhanced memory and learning capabilities, and even increased empathy and compassion.

By strengthening your mindfulness mental muscles, you will enhance your ability to think through situations, control impulses, and make decisions without becoming overwhelmed by anxiety or other distracting emotional responses. By using mindfulness to tap into present-moment awareness, you will learn to more rapidly activate your PFC (Tang et al., 2015), enabling you to pay attention to what matters most in the moment and make more rational decisions, rather than reacting from an emotional, amygdala-driven stance. You will therefore be better able to think, rather than feel your way through the stressful moments of your life and, in the process, to become a calmer, more grounded parent.

These neurological enhancements can have a profound impact on your functioning and life satisfaction as a parent. People who regularly engage in mindfulness exercises experience decreased anxiety, stress, and depression, greater feelings of happiness and satisfaction with their relationships, better sleep quality, and even better immune functioning. Imagine realizing all these benefits. How might your life look different? Maybe you envision yourself having more time and energy to be present with your kids, connect with your partner, and really take care of yourself. Let these possibilities for your future motivate you to continue the work you are putting into becoming a more mindful parent.

Time to Hit the Mindfulness Brain Gym

All mindfulness-based brain rewiring exercises involve the same active ingredient: the practice of making contact with your thoughts, feelings, and sensations, then gently bringing your attention back to the current moment. Note that some of the mindfulness exercises in this chapter and the ways you can incorporate them into your life take longer than others. Some you can do while walking down a busy street; others require a quiet place free of external distractions. Much like the different exercise equipment and classes at a gym, there are many different ways you can enhance your mindfulness mental circuitry.

What often gets in the way of our clients' engaging in mindfulness training is preconceived ideas of what mindfulness should be and how long they should practice. You've already read enough here to know about challenging rigid thoughts and expectations. You can move forward in this chapter with greater flexibility and self-compassion, knowing that wherever you are today is a great place to begin your mindfulness practice.

Give yourself the space to create this practice. First, set a realistic and feasible goal. We designed the mindfulness exercises in this chapter for busy parents like you. We doubt you have the time or emotional bandwidth for a weekend-long silent retreat, but we hope you can give yourself a few minutes a day to consistently exercise your mindfulness muscles. You and your loved ones deserve a more present, emotionally available, grounded version of you.

The first exercise will help you establish a brief daily mindfulness practice. Doing more is even better for your health; doing less can still be very helpful. You can practice in the morning, evening, or a different time each day, but know that setting a regular schedule seems to help some people.

Your mindfulness practice space should be simple but comfortable, in a place where you won't be interrupted by anyone else (we know, we know—this is probably a tall order). If possible, find somewhere you don't use for other things. This doesn't have to be a whole room. Most people have great success picking a small corner of their bedroom that they don't usually sit in, or maybe sitting in front of the window and looking out at a tree. You're setting up a special area just for your mindfulness training. Grab a cushion to sit on (or a chair, if it makes you more comfortable), and set a soothing object in your line of sight—maybe a stone you picked up on a hike, or a favorite figurine or candle. If you share a room, you can pack these away when you're done with your mindfulness training, then take them back out for your next session.

You are now ready to begin working out your mindfulness mental muscles.

Parent Brain Rewiring Exercise: An Introduction to Mindfulness

1. Set a timer for two minutes. When you first start engaging in mindfulness exercises, less can be more in terms of how many minutes you practice. This first baby step of working your mindfulness mental muscles can take you a long way.

2. Set your soothing object within view and take a seat in your mindfulness spot.

3. Gently rest your gaze on your object. You might part your lips slightly, letting breath flow smoothly in and out. Try to bring a completely nonjudgmental awareness to the object, perhaps viewing it as though you're an alien from another planet who has never seen such a thing before and therefore doesn't have all sorts of stories about it. Simply notice its shape and its colors, its shadows and angles.

4. Whenever you start to have judgments or thoughts, getting lost in stories about the past or the future, simply notice where your mind has gone, then bring it back to noticing the qualities of your object. Remember, you're learning to not try to block your thoughts, but to simply observe them, without judgment; to notice where your mind goes without getting carried away by distractions, always coming back to the present moment.

Expect the unexpected. When you engage in mindfulness exercises, whether with a guided recording or our instructions, you'll have all sorts of experiences. Some days your thoughts will seem like a storm, nearly unending and impossible to get out from under. Other days your thoughts and feelings will seem more like clouds that float by peacefully. Truly, there is no right or wrong experience. Everyone has stormy practices and practices that offer an oasis of calm. Just by showing up to your spot and practicing returning to the present moment—no matter how drenched in "mental rain" you may feel—you are rewiring your brain and realizing the benefits so many have gained from mindfulness training. In fact, your very stormiest sessions may ultimately bring the greatest rewiring benefits.

Remember, the essence of mindfulness training is not the elimination of uncomfortable thoughts and feelings but growing your ability to be here and now, noticing when your thoughts and feelings have wandered from the present and gently guiding them back to the current moment.

Enhance Your Brain's Discrimination Ability

As your brain scans for danger and threats, sometimes it misfires and decides you or your loved ones are in danger when you are safe. Mental noise is often your brain emitting false alarms, warning you of potential challenge zones.

Jenny, like most parents, has had some experience with mental noise flooding her brain when she wanted to simply enjoy her family. Sitting in the audience at Ava's piano recital, Jenny found the noise in her head growing loud, as thoughts circled about her son's social life. She began to replay carpool conversations in her head, asking herself if Ben would ever outgrow his shyness, even worrying about how he might fare in college if he didn't put himself out there more. As Jenny's worries grew, the situation in her mind felt more and more dire, her brain misfiring and emitting a false alarm about her son's well-being. Ben was sitting right next to her at the piano concert, safe and sound. Nothing about his social life required her immediate attention. She felt anxious and frustrated—anxious about her son's well-being and frustrated that on Ava's special day she was listening more to the thoughts in her head than the piano music that Ava had been practicing for so many months. Held captive by mental noise, Jenny felt incapable of being the present, supportive parent she wanted to be.

With the following exercise, Jenny (and countless parents like her) can catch mental noise as it arises and disengage from unhelpful false alarms, refocusing on the present moment.

Parent Brain Rewiring Exercise: Unhook and Reel Back to the Present Moment

For the next day, your goal is to practice unhooking from your mental noise as many times as possible. On an average day you may experience hundreds of intruding thoughts, attempting to pull you away from the current moment, to take you where they want to go. Sometimes you will be automatically swept up in these thoughts so rapidly that you'll have no chance to notice they have surfaced. Other times you may notice a few moments into the attentional detour. Still other times, you'll notice the mental noise just as it begins. All help you practice enhancing your mindfulness capabilities. Simply take the following steps to practice unhooking from your mental noise.

Note: Sometimes our clients write these instructions on a sticky note, make them a screensaver, or come up with a way to remind themselves to unhook from their mental noise throughout the day.

1. Practice noticing when mental noise surfaces and tries to hook you into its content and mission.

2. Practice unhooking from the mental noise by reminding yourself:

    • This thought may feel urgent, but you're actually safe and sound.

- There is no immediate threat or situation to be tended to—you have simply received BS mail and momentarily mistaken it for an urgent message.

3. Practice reeling yourself back to the current moment by gently but actively gathering your attention and returning it to whatever you were trying to accomplish before the mental noise surfaced.

4. When you're done, write down in your Training Journal any thoughts or key takeaways.

Here's Jenny's example:

1. Practice noticing hook: Why is my Ben always the quiet one in the carpool? It seems like all the kids are always talking over him. Do they not respect him? Or does he just not have anything interesting to say? Will the boys even want to stay friends with him when they all go off to high school? What if he gets left behind? What if one day he's completely socially isolated and never leaves his room anymore?

2. Practice unhooking: Right now, I am noticing my parent brain offering up scary thoughts about Ben's social functioning and about peer challenges he may have when he is a teenager.

3. Practice reeling back to the present moment: At this very moment, Ben is sitting in the back seat of my car. I am driving home from baseball practice, and as far as the eye can see there is no present danger. It's a calm, sunny day, and the traffic is light. We are safe and sound. I just got caught up in my thoughts and mistook my BS for truth. I will now bring my attention back to the current moment and appreciate this carpool for what it is.

Parent Brain Rewiring Exercise: The Undesirable Party Attendee

Imagine you are throwing a party and you've found out that your partner invited a colleague. He explains that this colleague is a key player in an upcoming project and it's important to make an effort to get to know him better outside of the office. Now imagine that you find this particular colleague to be rude, condescending, and not at all a person you would choose to chat with over a cocktail. Yikes. So now you have three choices: (1) tell your partner to uninvite this guest, (2) cancel your party to avoid seeing this person, or (3) nod and say hi when the person arrives and then focus on the people you do want to interact with. When you walk by this unwanted guest, you can give a quick smile of acknowledgment, but you don't have to stop and chat. You don't have to be rude or ignore him, but you don't have to give him too much attention either. This is how you need to treat the distracting thoughts and feelings that arise and attempt to pull you out of the present moment.

Try this:

1. Set a timer for five minutes.

2. For the next five minutes, put your attention on a task you need to accomplish, such as washing dishes, paying bills, or anything else on your to-do list.

3. Mindfully notice whenever a new thought, feeling, or sensation surfaces and pulls your attention away from the task at hand.

4. Practice giving a brief smile of acknowledgment to the less-than-desirable mental guest. Try to not argue, wrestle, or ignore it, but give it a quick "Hello, I see you have arrived" and then gently guide your attention back to the task you are working on.

5. When you're done, write down in your Training Journal any thoughts or key takeaways.

Quick Hacks for Extra Mindfulness

Starting (and maintaining) a mindfulness practice can be intimidating. It's important to remember that practicing mindfulness does not have to be time consuming or overwhelming. We know you're busy enough as it is! Here are a few quick hacks for seamlessly injecting mindfulness into your daily life.

Cue Yourself to Be Mindful

To remind yourself to practice mindfulness throughout your day, we recommend setting automatic reminders. You can set alarms or calendar events on your phone or strategically place handwritten reminders that you'll see throughout the day (a note on the coffee maker, in your wallet, on your bathroom mirror, and so on). When you see these reminders, gently bring your nonjudgmental attention to what is happening in your current moment and just notice your surroundings, checking in with all of your senses.

Mindfulness Mantras

A mantra—a word or phrase that you repeat to help you concentrate—can be a lifeline back to the present moment. It can hold special meaning or be a simple cue to engage your mindfulness muscles. Choose a mantra and write it down so you can easily remember it. The next time you are drifting away from the present moment, repeat your mantra until you return to the here and now.

Here are a few mindfulness mantras to try:

- Be here now.

- Disconnect and reconnect.

- False alarm.

- Brain spam, not critical info.

- Life is happening now.

- Return to the present.

Mindful Eating

The next time you eat, whether you're enjoying a meal with the family or thrown-together snacks on the go, try to do so mindfully. Work to tune out distractions and focus on the experience of taking in nutrition through food in the moment. Take each bite slowly, paying close attention to all the aspects of the food you are consuming: the texture, aroma, and flavor profile. Try not to judge the food as good or bad; simply describe it using all of your senses (crunchy, cold, salty, spicy, tart, and so on). As you thoroughly chew your food, you may even notice the taste changes as flavors are released.

Parent Brain Rewiring Exercise: Mindful Parenting

With your new understanding of mindfulness as a practice and the ways you can use your skills in everyday life, it's time to apply this to your life as a parent. You may not feel like a mindfulness expert yet—most of us aren't! Mindfulness is an ongoing practice that requires intention. But you now have a solid foundation for living in the present as a more mindful parent. When parenting as usual calls for jam-packed agendas, racing thoughts, and multitasking, mindful parenting calls for increased connection, fulfillment, and joy in the present with your child and family. Complete the following two-part exercise and really notice the difference in your experiences.

Part A

1. Sit down with your child and ask how their day is going.

2. Ask your child to simply speak for one minute about their day.

3. Partially attend to what your child is saying while at the same time attending to all other thoughts and feelings that show up. Feel free to think of what you need to get done, what else you've got going that day, whether this is a good use of your time, and so on.

Part B

1. Ask your child to continue telling you about their day for another minute.

2. This time, practice mindfully attending to what your child is saying.

3. When your thoughts and feelings surface and intrude on the present moment, notice and acknowledge the thoughts and feelings, then gently return your attention to your child and all that they are sharing with you.

Compare and contrast these two experiences in your Training Journal.

Bonus Exercises

- After you try the two-part exercise, ask your child to guess which mental state (mindless or mindful) was which.

- Reverse roles and have your child be the listener and you be the speaker. Have them either mindfully or mindlessly attend to you; then you guess which mental state was which. Together, discuss how it felt to be on the receiving end of mindful rather than mindless attention and how it felt to be the one providing either mindful or mindless attention.

Upon completing this exercise, write down in your Training Journal any thoughts or key takeaways.

Parent Brain Rewiring Exercise: Shifting Attention Between Foreground and Background

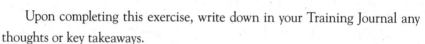

Take a moment to listen to the different sounds around you. Perhaps you hear the air conditioning system, the dryer tumbling in the other room, or your dog panting. Select one sound and give it all of your attention. Does it sound louder now that you are fully attending to it? How much was it catching your attention before you started this exercise?

Now pick an attention-requiring activity to engage in for one minute, such as reading or watching an interesting video on your phone. As you shifted your attention away from the background sound, did the volume seem fainter? As you directly placed your attention on a new stimulus, did the background sound appear louder or quieter?

You can apply the same concept to your mental noise. When you place all of your attention on your intruding thoughts and feelings, they will seem louder. When you place your attention on your present experience and whatever you want this moment to be about, these mental intrusions will fade into the background and become less and less noticeable.

Upon completing this exercise, write down in your Training Journal any thoughts or key takeaways.

Parent Brain Rewiring Exercise: Seeing versus Being Your Mental Noise

Learning to observe without overly engaging with mental noise will help you maximize your reserve of emotional energy to invest in the important parts of your life.

1. Write on a large sticky note a brain spam/mental noise message that you have recently experienced.

2. Place the sticky note over your eyes.

3. Notice how much of your visual field is blocked when you are overly engaged with your mental noise. What are you missing out on experiencing when you get fused with and locked into your BS?

4. Next, hold the sticky note with your BS message in your hand and extend that arm out with a gentle, expansive gesture.

5. How much of your visual field is blocked when you see the BS message from this arm's distance vantage point? Yes, the mental noise is still there, but what else can you see and attend to?

By engaging in these mindfulness exercises, you are rewiring your parent brain to operate with advanced attention-shifting abilities. You are now better able to *choose* where to place your attention instead of passively being dragged any which way by your overactive monkey mind. The more you practice mindfully noting your mental noise and then returning to the current moment, the more automatic this process will become.

How Mindfulness Exercises Rewire Your Parent Brain to Reduce Stress and Anxiety

By enhancing your parent brain's ability to be mindful, you are freeing it up to spend more time attending to the present moment. Practicing mindfulness decreases activity in your amygdala and increases engagement of your PFC—enhancing your ability to think clearly and make decisions in the present without being bogged down by anxiety or emotional reactivity. Parenthood demands so much of your time, energy, and attention; you deserve to get the most from the wonderful moments parenthood has to offer, instead of moving through life mindlessly with an endless stream of thoughts and feelings pulling you in countless directions. You don't have to wait for your to-do list to be shorter, the kids to be older, or life to be less busy to practice mindfulness. A more mindful parent brain embraces the present moment, no matter what the moment may be.

CHAPTER 5

Freedom from Your Past

Our next story contrasts two women whose parent brain default states developed very differently, based on the very different personal histories that had shaped them.

> Caroline and Amy were colleagues at the same law firm. They met as new associates, and over the years their relationship grew from coworkers to the closest of friends. Although they'd ended up in the same law firm, very different paths had led them to their current full-time jobs of lawyer and mom. Caroline came from a family of lawyers and high achievers; Amy was the first in her family to pursue a college degree. Their different life experiences colored the lenses through which Caroline and Amy viewed the world. So while they both worked 24/7 as lawyer and mom, they each had their own unique perspectives and experiences.

Caroline's Parent Brain Default State: Emotional Avoidance

Caroline came from a long line of perfectionists and high achievers. Her parents expressed their love by setting high expectations for Caroline and her siblings. They carted them from activity to activity, each child striving to be the best. From soccer and tennis to choir and debate team, Caroline required herself to excel. But there were still occasional moments when success eluded her. She remembers when her parents signed her up for violin lessons: no matter how hard she practiced, she could hardly distinguish between the notes. Her parents responded to this seeming failure with silent but soul-crushing looks of disappointment. They never directly told her she was "not good enough," but in their presence she always felt that she was somehow falling short. She told herself if she just kept trying she would eventually please them and stop feeling flawed. Over the years, Caroline put countless hours and an abundance of energy into trying to impress her parents and desperately sought to avoid their negative judgment.

Overall, Caroline's hard work and dedication to achievement served her well. She was a successful lawyer; the mother of two smart, conscientious children; and wife of a husband who adored her. Caroline's life operated like a well-oiled machine, and she was in charge of keeping it that way. Yet a gnawing sense of unease crept in whenever she paused for a rare break from hyperproductivity. It felt as though chaos resided below the pristine surface of her life. She feared that if she reflected on this for too long, she would get sucked into the emotional undertow, and the life she had worked so hard to create for herself and her family would end. She kept reminding herself to put one foot in front of the other, and the hard feelings would pass.

Caroline continued to outrun her uncomfortable thoughts and feelings and made every effort to maintain the aura of perfection that surrounded her family. One Sunday night at 10 p.m., after a fun-filled weekend, Caroline's thirteen-year-old daughter began to have an emotional meltdown. Caroline watched from the kitchen as Lucy stood over a poster board and rifled through stacks of paper, glue, and scissors spread out on the dining room table. As Lucy alternated between heavy sighs and audible whimpers, Caroline became flushed, sweaty, and on edge. Lucy had put off this science project for weeks. She was so busy with clubs, extracurriculars, and social events that she hardly had time to address her science project. Caroline was reminded of herself in middle school—overscheduled, overcommitted, and hanging onto perfection by a thread.

Lucy suddenly shouted "I can't do this!" and fell into a dining room chair, sweeping a pile of papers to the floor with a dramatic gesture. She began to sob into her hands. Caroline rushed into the dining room and wrapped her arms around her. Through her sobs, Lucy explained that the project was due by first period on Monday and was never going to get done in time at this rate.

"I just can't handle this, I really can't," she cried. Caroline felt sick to her stomach as she attempted to comfort Lucy, remembering how she'd felt when she was younger, working around the clock to get everything done and always be the best. It pained her deeply to see her daughter in such distress. She felt a strong motherly urge to rescue her.

"You know what, sweetie? Why don't you head upstairs and get to bed, okay? I'll handle this from here," she said, wiping away Lucy's tears. Within moments, the tears stopped flowing and Lucy headed upstairs, trusting that her poster board would be complete in time for first period. Caroline stayed up until 2 a.m. gluing construction paper onto her daughter's project.

As Caroline sat at the dining room table burning the midnight oil, thoughts about what had just transpired flooded her mind. On the one hand, she felt incredible relief after rescuing her daughter from such a moment of distress—the way Lucy's tears had dissipated when she swooped in to help felt like magic. At the same time, Caroline couldn't shake the feeling that rescuing Lucy might not have been the best decision. She wondered if it actually sent the message that Lucy couldn't handle challenges and needed to be saved by others. While Caroline wanted to ease her daughter's pain and shield her from difficulties, she also wanted her to build resilience and trust that she could handle what life throws her way. As she sifted through these thoughts and feelings, Caroline wondered how much of her own experience of being overscheduled and overwhelmed as a child contributed to her desire to save her daughter from that momentary pain.

Amy's Parent Brain Default State: Emotional Acceptance

Amy's path to becoming both lawyer and mom had not been easy. Amy's parents were loving but relatively absent, frequently taking extra shifts at work to make ends meet. When they got home after those grueling hours, they rarely had any emotional energy left for Amy's needs. Faced with a home life that could spare little to coddle or even tend to her, Amy always made it a priority to be self-sufficient. She worked hard at school, built her own social world, and strived to not put any additional burdens on her exhausted parents.

Extracurricular activities were rarely an option for Amy, as the money and time needed to invest in anything more than school alone were scarce. She had always loved softball, though, and her parents worked hard to give her the opportunity to play the game at school. She had never been on any travel teams or gone to the special camps or clinics that many other softball players had at her age—she simply played on the public school's team during the season. As she grew older, the disadvantage she faced grew more and more apparent, as the other girls on the team seemed to be developing skills much faster, thanks to time and money invested outside of the regular season. Amy remembers the widening gap between her passion for the game and her actual skill set. She still remembers the painful feelings of self-doubt and shame as her teammates and opponents all seemed to be able to outperform her.

Amy's son had been playing soccer for years. As he grew older and more opportunities unfolded in the soccer world, Amy was always there to register him for camps, clinics, and travel teams—everything she had missed out on in her own childhood. When her son's freshman year of high school rolled around and it was time for soccer tryouts, Amy held her breath. She had invested so much time, energy, and, frankly, finances in her son's soccer career, trying to close the gap in skills between her son and the other players that she worried was looming.

On the last day of tryouts, she parked her car and waited anxiously for her son to walk off the field and out to the parking lot. As she watched the other players trickling out into the parking lot with white envelopes in hand, she tried to read the expressions on their faces, wondering which player had received a congratulatory letter and which had received a gut-wrenching denial letter.

Her heart sank when she saw her son walking toward the car—the way he was looking down and dragging his feet was a dead giveaway. When he got into the passenger seat, no words were necessary. She watched as tears welled up in his eyes and he bit his lip; the sting of the bad news was fresh and painful for both of them. Amy felt her chest tighten, and her mind begin to race. She began mentally drafting a nasty email to the head coach. She thought about calling the principal to complain about the horrible politics of the soccer program. Amy noticed these thoughts flooding her brain and took a deep breath. She remembered how the sport she loved had left her feeling crushed and lonely in her later teenage years. She also remembered how she managed to get through the experience and grow from it, without needing anyone to rescue or save her. Amy knew that she needed to believe the same resilience was possible for her own son.

She took another deep breath and turned to her son. "You're gonna get through this, bud," she said lovingly. "I know you've got what it takes, and I'm here for you, okay?"

For the rest of the ride home, Amy sat with the urge to rescue her son and reminded herself that he did not need rescuing—he was capable of tolerating this momentary pain and moving through this challenging moment. Amy knew it was her role to be there for him and support him through this time, rather than being reactive and chasing fast relief from these feelings of anguish. She also recognized the ways her son reminded her of herself. He was passionate, athletic, determined—and hurt in this moment. It was a feeling Amy had known and moved through in her own journey as an athlete. She trusted that both her son's disappointment and her own emotional distress would pass. Her life experiences had taught her that struggling through challenging times is never fun, but it can offer important lessons in resiliency and inner strength.

Both Caroline and Amy were committed to supporting their children and felt a strong desire to protect them from any and all potential suffering. Caroline's early life experiences, filled with high expectations and conditional love, led her to rescue her daughter from the momentary distress of a procrastinated school project, rather than trusting that her daughter could cope with the challenge and learn and grow from it. Amy felt a similar sense of anxiety when her son faced rejection from the school's soccer team. Although she felt the urge to be reactive and take action against those involved in her son's difficult experience, Amy used this as an opportunity to remind herself of the resilience of both herself and her son. She trusted that just as she has moved through difficult moments in her own life, her son could do the same. Amy was committed to supporting her son wholeheartedly in all areas of life and understood that hardships and challenges are a part of living a meaningful life.

Learning to Manage Your Emotional Pain

There's a good chance that you've already done your best to move past any and all remaining emotional baggage from your childhood. You, like many people, have likely tried to go over, under, or around your emotional pain. Some painful moments are easier to move through than others. Even if you've tried, you may have found it difficult to really get past some painful memories. It's not that you haven't tried hard enough to escape the confines of your past; rather, you may actually be overdoing your efforts to do so.

With the skills you will learn through the exercises in this chapter, you can stop working so hard to avoid triggers from your past and their accompanying hard feelings, and you'll have more time and energy for living your best life today. Similar to how Amy was able to notice and then move through her own historic feelings of shame and embarrassment when they surfaced, you too can learn to identify, tolerate, and then move beyond yours. Through this hard work, you will be able to show up more fully for yourself, your children, and everyone and everything you value in your life today.

This chapter will help you learn to:

- Open up to, learn from, and then move past your historic pain points

- Enhance your ability to distinguish between a historic and a current threat

- Signal to your amygdala that you are not actually in danger when you stumble upon a historic pain point

- Make decisions in line with what you want your life to be about rather than what you want to avoid

- Experience enhanced resiliency as you teach your parent brain just how strong and emotionally hardy you truly are

Life's Inescapable Historic Pain Points

To be human is to inevitably experience some degree of emotional pain. We will all experience loss, disappointments, and soul-crushing blows. As discussed in chapter 3, the human brain (unlike any other animal's) has advanced thinking, reviewing, and assessing capabilities. Thanks to your PFC, you can plan for your future needs based on the key learnings from your prior life experiences, however painful. Your PFC's advanced thinking skills allow you to reflect on your past, then consider the implications for your future. Along with the benefits of this kind of creative problem solving, there are some costs in the form of reflecting and reviewing emotionally painful memories. This chapter will guide you through identifying, processing, and moving through those historic pain points to help you live more fully in the present. We'll work on increasing the accuracy of your brain's sensitivity to and interpretation of past pain points, so they no longer interrupt your ability to live in the present and enjoy life.

Stress, Memories, and the Brain

When you're experiencing a threatening event, such as trying out for a sports team or completing a high-stress assignment, the stress hormones pulsating through your body can temporarily disrupt your hippocampus's ability to process and store the event. The high-anxiety event may then be stored as an implicit rather than explicit memory. Implicit memories are stored as feelings, thoughts, and sensations but without conscious awareness of all aspects of the event. Explicit memories are more autobiographical; you can recall and speak to the details of the event in an integrated fashion (Siegel, 2020). For example, think about a low-stress moment you've experienced with your child—say, eating breakfast together and discussing weekend plans. Now think of a high-stress moment with your child—say, a time you urgently called their doctor to report troubling symptoms and determine whether you needed to go to the ER. Notice how the quality of these memories varies. The memory of discussing weekend plans with your child may surface as a mini movie, complete with sound and imagery. The memory of deciding whether you needed to take your child to the ER may be more fragmented and jarring. You may remember a few things said and a few images, and your body may react more intensely to this memory: shallower breathing, tensed shoulders, and a sudden sense of dread.

When implicit memories intrude, you may have a surprisingly disproportionate reaction to a current situation. You feel all sorts of big, uncomfortable emotions, although rationally you realize you are probably overreacting. For example, Caroline's PFC knew that her daughter's procrastinating on an assignment and potentially even turning it in late would not be the end of the world, yet her amygdala reacted as though her child needed saving from grave danger. When there is a disconnect between what your PFC thinks is true and what your amygdala feels is true, you have likely stirred up an implicit memory of a challenging moment that you haven't yet fully processed and made sense of. Your amygdala believes you are still experiencing an active threat. Even if your PFC attempts to convince your amygdala it's overreacting, your amygdala will always win. When survival is at stake, your action-oriented amygdala is always more powerful than your pontificating PFC. Which seems reasonable—unless the survival assessment is wrong.

If you or your children were in a burning building, would you want your PFC running the show, pointing out all of the pros and cons of the different safety routes, or would you want your amygdala to superpower you up so you can grab your children and flee the danger as rapidly as possible? The issue is the degree of risk. Every moment of life our survival is at stake. We cannot guarantee what the next moment will bring, so we must learn to tolerate the low-level threat present in each moment of life. Imagine living with your amygdala chronically activated, pointing out every potential threat you and your loved ones might encounter. How fun does that sound? There's not much room for listening to your child's laughter or snuggling on the couch together watching your favorite show if you are always on high alert for all the dangers your family may face.

Past Intruding on Present

Implicit memories of high-stress moments are bound to arise sometimes. And this can certainly be for the good. Imagine driving your daughter and her friend home from school. You overhear your child say she is thinking of joining the student council, and her friend points out how "uncool" student council is. Your daughter retorts, "I was kidding! I wouldn't *actually* do student council." You begin to feel a heaviness in your chest and feelings of sadness. You flash back to your younger self standing in front of a bulletin board, debating whether you should sign up for an activity but, considering potential social implications, giving up what you wanted, just to try to please other people. Perhaps once you're back at home you share with your daughter your thoughts about allowing fear of other people's judgment to cause you to miss out on exciting or interesting activities. You let her know you will respect whatever decision she makes and that you appreciate her listening.

In this situation, you have learned, from your own difficult moments, to more effectively manage your current and future life. But intruding implicit memories can also be unhelpful and burdensome, such as when Caroline's own painful memories led her to rescue her daughter from what might have otherwise been a growing opportunity.

This chapter is here to help your PFC apply conscious attention to undigested historic pain points. Your PFC's open, unflinching gaze can transform implicit memories from murky, unclear internal messaging to user-friendly information in the form of explicit memories. By engaging your PFC to observe and connect with those pain points, you teach your amygdala that these difficult moments happened in your past and are no longer associated with an active threat. Your amygdala will come to understand that right now you and your loved ones are safe and sound, so it can save its energy reserve for real danger.

Your amygdala will no longer need to sound an alarm whenever you encounter situations it associates with a past threat. When you are no longer impaired by fight-flight-freeze stress hormones and emotions, you're better equipped to manage such challenges. Your brain can use relevant lessons to help you move through present and future challenges, rather than getting caught up in an unresolved emotional response. Now you can gain wisdom and guidance from your historic pain points.

Distress Tolerance for Two

It's not easy to address difficult memories and feel painful emotions. If you've been running from your historic pain points for years, it might be hard to imagine taking the time and energy to move through and past them. Check in with yourself and consider your *why*. Why did you pick up this book and decide to take the next steps to become a more mindful, grounded parent? Many parents we work with include themselves and their own well-being in their 'why'; others mention their children and families. Working to process your historic pain points will benefit not only you, but your children and family as well.

By addressing, processing, and moving past your historic pain points, you enable yourself to live a more grounded, emotionally regulated life. When something that was once triggering no longer elicits the same highly emotional reaction, you can act calmly and rationally in situations that once sent your anxiety through the roof. When your child observes their parent behaving calmly and rationally (even in the face of a stressful or anxiety-provoking situation), they have a better chance of behaving calmly and rationally as well. Your calm, grounded response communicates your confidence in their ability to handle the situation and your belief in the resilience of yourself, your child, and your family. This gives all of you permission to face the situation and proceed with bravery and resilience rather than fear and avoidance.

Over time, your distress tolerance abilities will reinforce your child's belief in their own abilities. They too will learn that even when something is hard or painful, they can move through the moment and tolerate whatever emotions come up, trusting that they are resilient enough to endure.

Right now, take a moment to close your eyes and envision each member of your family (yourself included) feeling calm, confident, and capable. Imagine what it will be like to see your strong, resilient child believing in themselves (even in the difficult moments) the same way you believe in them. As you move through this chapter, allow this vision to fuel your efforts and guide your path forward.

Hardwired to Avoid Discomfort

So far this all may sound simple enough. All you need to do is make contact with your historic pain points, and your amygdala will no longer misfire and mistake a past threat for a current danger. So why haven't you already done this? Why are there still so many painful memories you work so hard to avoid thinking about? Truthfully, there is nothing intuitive about actively seeking out opportunities to expose yourself to painful moments from your past. It is natural to *avoid* contact with pain, whether physical or emotional. Your brain is hardwired to reward you for seeking out situations that make you feel good and safe—and to encourage you to avoid uncomfortable and potentially dangerous situations.

The neurotransmitter in your brain known as dopamine plays a role in motivating you to seek what's comfortable, safe, and satisfying and avoid what's uncomfortable, dangerous, and dissatisfying. Your brain is always experiencing, learning, and then reminding you of what it finds rewarding—or uncomfortable—and encourages you to move toward pleasure over pain. When you're in an uncomfortable situation and choose to retreat, dopamine rewards you by flooding your brain with this feel-good chemical.

This all sounds relatively fair and effective. What could possibly be the downside? Here's the problem: when your brain is flooded with dopamine, it is much harder for your PFC to kick in with its logical thinking. So, in a dopamine-induced state, you'll be more likely to mistake a false alarm for a truly dangerous situation. And the more situations your brain determines are dangerous, the more it will see you as vulnerable. The more your brain thinks you're compromised, the more often and intensely it will sound the danger alarm, and the more stress and anxiety you'll experience. Unfortunately, this process feeds negative beliefs about yourself and the world around you. After enough dopamine-fueled avoidance, you may come to believe false messages about your inability to manage challenging situations and life's inevitable pain points.

What You Resist, Persists

Imagine a damp, dark basement where you store old photo albums. Now imagine that instead of photo albums filled with pictures and memorabilia of life's most joyful moments, these albums are filled with reminders of the most painful memories. Every day you walk by the door of the basement and think *It's too scary and terrible to go down there. If I went down there and saw those photo albums filled with awful memories, I would never recover.* Now imagine the basement door is right next to the kitchen. Whenever you enter or exit your kitchen, you are reminded that whatever you do, you must not go down into the basement.

If this was your kitchen and your basement and your albums, would you be able to avoid thinking about those difficult times from your past? You might think there is an easy solution: just go down to the basement and move the albums, so you won't have to be haunted by your past. And you are correct! That is exactly what this chapter will help you accomplish. You will go down into your brain's basement; make contact with the albums of thoughts, feelings, and memories of your intruding historic pain points; and find a new place to store them that does not require so much emotional energy to avoid.

Parent Brain Rewiring Exercise: Assessing the Impact of Your Historic Pain Points

Review this list of sentiments people commonly feel when their historic pain points are impacting their present, and in your Training Journal note any you agree with.

- Painful experiences from my past make it difficult for me to live my life to the fullest.

- Upsetting thoughts or images associated with past painful moments pop into my head and pull me away from the present.

- I occasionally have bad dreams or nightmares about past difficult moments.

- Sometimes I feel like I am reliving and still stuck in a painful moment.

- I can quickly get upset or anxious when I am reminded of certain difficult moments.

- With these reminders, I can have a physical reaction such as increased heart rate, sweating, or body tension.

- I try not to think about difficult memories, to avoid the emotional discomfort that comes with them.

- Sometimes I avoid activities, people, or places that remind me of painful memories.

If you answered "yes" to any of the above items, difficult memories may be preventing you from living your present and future life to the fullest.

Obtaining the Right Level of Assistance

We humans inevitably must navigate some adversity. Sometimes we can do the work of moving past emotional challenge zones on our own or with a helpful book as a guide and companion, such as this one (if we may say so). Other times we deserve a bit of extra support from the sidelines. If painful memories from your past frequently intrude on your present life, cause you emotional distress, and negatively impact your performance in key aspects of your life, you may benefit from meeting with a therapist to share the work of healing from your historical pain points. Seeking help is not a sign of weakness or failure. Far from it! Everyone can benefit from therapy at some point in their life. When mental health symptoms reach a moderate to severe level, recovery will progress faster with a trained professional's coaching you through and soon past the pain.

Moving Past Your Past

Similar to wanting to lose weight and then only talking and thinking about joining a gym, you can't lighten the emotional weight of your historical pain points by only talking or thinking about them. It requires action, bringing PFC-oriented attention to bear. By intentionally making contact with the thoughts, feelings, and sensations associated with difficult memories, you teach your brain that you are now safe and sound. You no longer live through the threatening moments when these uncomfortable thoughts and feelings were originally generated.

When implicit memories associated with historical pain points continue to intrude, your brain believes you are still in danger. So it assumes you must not let your guard down and must stay on the lookout for associated threats. The exercises throughout this chapter will teach your parent brain that your pain points were challenging and distressing, but you survived them and can stand down your high alert. By consciously focusing on painful memories associated with these pain points, you prompt your hippocampus to encode this information to create adaptive and more accurate explicit memories. You gain a new, empowered perspective on your early-life pain and suffering. Through this hard work, your brain will be better able to differentiate a current threat that needs attention from lingering associations with past experiences.

Enhancing Your Power of Observation

It's important to enhance your awareness of when implicit memories intrude on the present. Intentionally paying attention to or "tracking" your historical pain points will help you flip your role from prisoner of this emotional pain to detective trying to solve a case. The following parent brain rewiring exercise will help you become a more astute observer of your intruding historical pain points.

Parent Brain Rewiring Exercise: Know Your Tendencies and Patterns

1. Over the next few days, use your Training Journal to track any intrusive, uncomfortable thoughts, feelings, or sensations. To get the most out of this activity, it is best to focus on the uncomfortable internal experiences that cause you the greatest distress. Feel free to track only the ones you observe to cause you a distress rating of 5 or above (on a scale of 0 to 10). Include the following tracking data:

- Date/Time:

- Situation:

- Thought(s):

- Feeling(s):

- Sensation(s):

- Emotional distress level: ____/10

- Estimate of emotional distress level for average person: ____/10

2. Once you've logged the data and rated your distress on a scale of 0 to 10, make your best guess as to the level of emotional distress you imagine the average person would experience in this very same scenario, on a scale of 0 to 10.

3. If there is a gap between the emotional distress you are experiencing and the average person's experience, chances are this is an intruding historical pain point.

By becoming aware of your frequent thoughts, feelings, and sensations from your past, you can pinpoint the implicit memories you most need to address. Here is an example of Caroline's intruding historical pain points log:

- Date/Time: 7/19 @ 2 p.m.

- Situation: Important work meeting with my boss

- Thought(s): My boss thinks I'm unprepared and don't know what I'm talking about

- Feeling(s): Terrified, nervous, jumpy

- Sensation(s): Tension in my head, difficulty taking deep breaths, hands feeling cold/tingly

- Emotional distress level: 7/10

- Estimate of emotional distress level for average person: 4/10

- Date/Time: 7/21 @ 4 p.m.

- Situation: Dropping daughter off at tutoring

- Thought(s): *She didn't do any of her studying and is completely unprepared, and now her tutor can tell that she's not dedicated enough to the tutoring program*

- Feeling(s): Worried, embarrassed, stressed

- Sensation(s): Cloudy headed, tension in my head

- Emotional distress level: 6/10

- Estimate of emotional distress level for average person: 2/10

Reflect

- Any common themes in your emotional distress?

- Any connections between your thoughts, feelings, and sensations?

- Any triggering times of day or specific situations?

- Any memories that keep showing up for you?

Exposure and Response Prevention (ERP)

It's time to teach your amygdala that the thoughts, feelings, and sensations associated with your historical pain points are uncomfortable, but not dangerous. You will use the powerful CBT technique of exposure and response prevention (ERP). ERP entails gradually confronting feared thoughts, feelings, sensations, and external stimuli while disengaging from any avoidance or safety behaviors. The goal is to *intentionally* evoke anxiety and discomfort through contact with a feared stimuli and teach your brain through experience that it can tolerate the associated discomfort. Your parent brain will also learn that although uncomfortable, these thoughts, feelings, and sensations are not dangerous and need not be avoided at all costs.

You may feel alarmed by these tactics. We get it—who wouldn't be hesitant to engage in exercises that intentionally bring on emotional discomfort? But we know that you are already probably feeling uncomfortable and bothered by your intruding historical pain points. And the more you push those away, the more they will keep intruding. With ERP, you decide how and when you'll cue up these uncomfortable thoughts, feelings, and sensations yourself. Years of research on ERP have demonstrated that it is highly effective for decreasing emotional distress associated with intruding internal experiences (Fabricant et al., 2013).

Building a More Resilient Brain

To break this cycle of emotional distress about emotional distress, you must teach your brain that there is nothing dangerous or catastrophic about having uncomfortable thoughts or feelings. When you disengage from emotional avoidance and other control strategies, you allow yourself to directly experience painful thoughts and emotions. This teaches your brain that thoughts, feelings, and images are not dangerous. You can rewire your brain to learn how to observe, experience, and soon move past emotional discomfort.

By learning to tolerate emotional discomfort rather than avoid it, you not only waste less energy engaging in a fruitless battle against yourself, but you also gain a more resilient brain. With practice, you'll gain access to a richer, more satisfying life, as you no longer need to avoid life's bumpy roads. Buckle up for a new kind of ride that helps you navigate unexpected potholes and changing weather conditions, as you seek out meaning, adventure, and a life on your own terms.

Learning What You Can Handle

From early in life, your genetic makeup and your learned experiences both influence how you react to discomfort or new situations. If you grew up in an environment where you were gently pushed and encouraged to work your way through age-appropriate challenges, you may have already been doing the hard work of teaching your brain it can handle being uncomfortable. In contrast, if you grew up in an environment where you were frequently "rescued" from situations that your brain considered too difficult or one where you were pushed too aggressively to "get over it," not acknowledging your discomfort, you may have had fewer opportunities to effectively grow your resilience capabilities.

No matter your starting point, it's time now to teach your brain just how hardy and competent it is. The first step in rewiring your brain to become more resilient is to remind it and yourself of how much discomfort you already move through daily. It's common to vilify emotional pain as something that is unbearable and must be avoided at all costs. But like physical pain, emotional pain is intended to signal that something noteworthy occurred and you should proceed with caution. From this viewpoint, consider how much discomfort you've been able to handle throughout your life and what this tells you about your ability to manage life's less-than-ideal moments.

Parent Brain Rewiring Exercise: You Can Handle Discomfort

Find somewhere quiet where you can really focus on this rewiring. Now think of all of the uncomfortable feelings you experience frequently. Have you experienced any of the following within the past month?

- Feeling hot or cold

- Paper cut

- Headache or migraine

- Stubbed toe

- Bumped head

- Cold or flu

- Broken or sprained bone

- Food poisoning

- Getting a shot

- Dental work

- Discomfort during or after a hard workout

Were you strong enough to tolerate the discomfort of these feelings and move forward with your life?

Next time you stub your toe or have any other form of physical discomfort, scan your body and really hone in on what it feels like to have these difficult feelings. And the next time you feel emotional pain, do the same. How are the feelings different? How are they the same? Reflect on your main takeaways in your Training Journal.

When you learn to recognize emotional pain as just another category of discomfort, one that you might manage daily, you will start to build on your emotional resilience capabilities. You teach your brain to neither fear emotional discomfort nor treat it as too powerful to be challenged. You're rewiring your brain to see emotional discomfort as just another form of incoming data that can teach you something and help you move forward more effectively.

Inaccurate Beliefs About Emotional Distress

It is common to feel more equipped to handle physical discomfort than emotional discomfort. Our clients often say they'd rather deal with painful physical conditions than continue to endure painful emotions such as fear, sadness, or shame. In a recent session, one said, "If only I had a broken leg or maybe even some sort of heart issue instead. Anything would be better than feeling this fear and impending doom."

If you fear and avoid emotional discomfort more than physical discomfort, it's likely you hold unhelpful and inaccurate beliefs about the experience of emotional pain. Often these thoughts assume the worst about your emotional pain resilience, which then saps your motivation and confidence to take on all that life offers. You are left feeling stuck in your pain and further away from the important things that make life worth living. This may lead you to miss out on precious moments with your children and family. For example, the new parent who is too anxious to attend a play group with their toddler misses out on the opportunity to bond with their little one and connect with other parents in the community. The parent who feels overwhelmed by stress at the dinner table may be too "in their own head" to be fully present for laughter and connection with their children and partner.

Perhaps your own beliefs about emotional distress have pulled you out of the present moment or led you to question your ability to handle a situation. Read the following list and note whether you hold (or have held in the past) any of these common (but inaccurate) beliefs about emotional distress:

- I am still feeling pain from the past; how could I handle more?

- I just barely made it through all that pain only because so much time has passed.

- If I let myself truly feel this, I'm going to totally lose control.

- I won't be able to function or cope if I allow myself to feel this pain.

- I'm not going to survive this.

- I can't handle it.

- The pain is unbearable.

- I will never feel better.

- The discomfort will never end.

- Others will judge me as weak for feeling so bad.

- I can't be around other people when I am feeling this bad.

The challenge with holding these beliefs is that they enhance your amygdala's fear response to any situation that may bring on uncomfortable emotions. As we know, if you perceive a situation as dangerous, anxiety is triggered in the brain. So if we perceive that not only is the situation dangerous, but so is our emotional response to the situation (*Oh no, I hate parent-teacher conferences; they make me so anxious, and I can't handle feeling anxious like that; it's completely unbearable!*), the amygdala's fear response is heightened and our overall distress increases. When your PFC sends untrue messages to your amygdala about your ability to manage emotional distress, the amygdala reacts fearfully, assuming you must be in danger. After all, why else would you be internally screaming something along the lines of *I can't handle this feeling!* Something must be really, really bad.

Parent Brain Rewiring Exercise: Challenge Your Inaccurate Beliefs About Emotional Discomfort

It's time to start offering yourself a more realistic assessment of just how bad it *really* is to experience emotional distress, no matter your life's pain points. By shifting to a view of uncomfortable thoughts and feelings as unpleasant but survivable, you will harness the power of your PFC to calm down your trigger-happy amygdala. Instead of your PFC telling your amygdala, *You can't handle this emotionally painful moment—remember all the other times it felt so bad?* it will instead tell it, *This is hard, and you will get through it, just like you have done before.*

For the next day, notice and record in your Training Journal the thoughts your brain offers up when experiencing anxiety about an upcoming emotionally challenging event.

1. Describe the distressing situation.

2. Observe and then write down all thoughts associated with your inaccurate beliefs about emotional discomfort.

3. Rate your overall distress level on a scale of 0 to 10.

4. Provide a realistic and balanced thought that challenges your inaccurate belief.

5. Rate your distress level on a scale of 0 to 10.

Here is Caroline's example:

1. Situation: I was thinking about the PTA meeting at the kids' school.

2. Catastrophic belief about emotional discomfort: It's going to be so awkward. I won't have anything to say to the other parents, and I'll end up feeling panicked and trapped there. It will be awful.

3. Distress Level (0–10): 9/10

4. Realistic, balanced counterthought: *Every time I have to go to one of these school events, I always dread them and picture myself being completely awkward with the other parents. Even though I always think they're going to be totally unbearable, they pretty much always turn out fine. Not much fun, but definitely not so bad that I can't handle it.*

5. New Distress Level (0–10): 5/10

After one week, come back to this exercise and reflect:

- How did you feel when you accepted your catastrophic beliefs about emotional discomfort?

- How did you feel after you offered yourself a more balanced, realistic assessment of your ability to tolerate and survive the upcoming emotional distress?

- Did your amygdala calm down once your PFC began to offer less gloom-and-doom predictions of your ability to survive the challenges before you?

Short-Term Pain, Long-Term Gain

As CBT practitioners, we are big fans of tolerating a bit of short-term pain (more like discomfort, but that does not rhyme with 'gain') for a whole lot of long-term gain. That is exactly what the powerful tool of ERP gives you—a lifetime of long-term gain in the form of freedom from your historical pain points.

Let's say you want to start swimming regularly to get into better shape, but the water feels uncomfortably cold when you lower your body into the pool. You could retreat from the water, wrap up in a warm towel, and read a book instead of working out. You'll probably feel better in the moment, but you won't get any healthier physically. The other option is to jump in, tolerate the initial shock of the cold water, and soon acclimate as you get moving toward your goal of improving your physical fitness.

Note: Although you can engage in exposure tasks on your own, it may be helpful to have a therapist who specializes in ERP by your side to help you creatively tailor exposures, provide accountability and encouragement, and set you up for success.

Parent Brain Rewiring Exercise: Making Contact with Your Historic Pain Points

This is a reflective journaling exercise. You'll need ten to fifteen uninterrupted minutes to write your answers to the following reflection questions in your Training Journal.

First, find a comfortable space where you won't be disturbed. We know that approaching an exercise that asks you to think about painful experiences in the past can feel daunting. Gently remind your parent brain that although it may be uncomfortable, it is not dangerous.

Set a timer for one minute, then close your eyes. Conjure up an image of yourself as a young child. Think about your younger self and any painful emotional or physical experiences you endured. It doesn't matter if others may not have considered it a traumatic experience; if it was painful for you, then you are at the right place for this exercise. Just observe your younger self in that situation. What are you doing? Where are you? Try to see the expression on your face. Scan the image that surfaces to note any additional details.

Reflect on your experience in your Training Journal:

- What did you notice about your experience—could you open up to it, or was your brain trying to avoid it?

- How did it feel to go back in time and intentionally think about and make room for this difficult moment in your life?

Next, draw a picture of any imagery that comes to mind when you think of this emotionally painful moment from your past. This does not have to be a work of art; it is simply a way to make contact with this historic pain.

- What images surfaced as you drew out this memory?

- Scan your body, from your head through your stomach down to your toes. What sensations do you notice in your body as you make contact with your past? Do you feel any heaviness? Where are you holding tension? Can you tolerate and make a teeny tiny bit of room for this emotional discomfort?

Parent Brain Rewiring Exercise: Expose Yourself to "Painful" Words

1. Write a list of ten words that come to mind when you think about painful moments from your childhood.

2. For each word, rate on a scale of 0 to 10 how anxious each word or phrase makes you.

3. For any word you rated greater than 0 in eliciting anxiety, say the word a hundred times out loud. Note how anxious you are feeling before you do the exposure exercise, and how anxious you feel after.

Here's part of Amy's example:

Lonely: Pre-exposure 6/10, post-exposure 3/10

Lost: Pre-exposure 5/10, post-exposure 3/10

Scared: Pre-exposure 6/10, post-exposure 3/10

Confused: Pre-exposure 7/10, post-exposure 2/10

Unloved: Pre-exposure 7/10, post-exposure 3/10

Parent Brain Rewiring Exercise: Expose Yourself to Your "Painful" Story

1. Find a quiet, private place to be alone for a few minutes. Sometimes quiet, private places are hard to come by for parents, but you are worth taking the time to find one for this important brain rewiring work.

2. Think of a specific moment in your childhood that was particularly painful. Think back to the way it looked, sounded, and felt. With this memory in mind, write a brief story outlining the events of this painful experience. Think of it like a movie, describing in detail what it was like to be you in that moment. It can be as long or as short as you like, but we recommend keeping it under one minute long.

3. With the story of your painful memory on paper, use your smartphone or another recording device to record yourself reading this story aloud. Notice your anxiety level the first time you read the story aloud. Rate it on a scale of 0 to 10.

4. Listen to the recording and notice how you are feeling in your body. Where is your anxiety level now? Listen to this story on repeat until your anxiety level has dropped by half or more.

Parent Brain Rewiring Exercise: Expose Yourself to a Fuller Life

1. Think about the situations and environments you find yourself avoiding to escape the discomfort of your past pain. This could include the avoidance of places, people, situations, and so on.

2. List these situations and rate each on a scale of 0 to 10, with 10 being the most avoided.

3. Choose one situation that is mildly to moderately anxiety-provoking (preferably rated at or below 5/10) and make a plan for when and how you will face it. Think through what it might be like. For example:

- *Situation:* Making small talk with other parents on the sidelines of our kids' sports game and feeling nervous, socially awkward, and uncomfortable.

- *Plan:* Next Saturday at Jacob's baseball tournament, I will place my lawn chair next to the other parents, instead of farther away. I can commit myself to chatting with the other parents for at least the first three innings. Even if I feel awkward and don't have much to say, I will be present for the interaction and tolerate the discomfort. I know I can handle it.

Once you've tackled one item on your list, you can begin to work your way through the rest, moving from low-anxiety to high-anxiety items, as if climbing a ladder. Each time you successfully face a situation without avoiding it, you're rewiring your parent brain.

You can expect to feel some anxiety when you face these situations. The goal is not to be without fear, but to live a full, valued life in the face of fear, proving to yourself that you truly can handle anything.

Customizing Your ERP Plan

Exposing yourself to your historical pain points in a systematic, organized fashion allows your brain to deactivate the emotional reactivity that pulses through these relics from your past. By creating and implementing an ERP training plan customized for you, you will gradually confront historical pain points at a pace that feels like a challenge to you—not too easy, not too hard.

Parent Brain Rewiring Exercise: Create Your Own Exposure Hierarchy

An exposure hierarchy is a step-by-step plan that breaks down your fears (in this case, your intruding historical pain points) into actionable, measurable behavioral targets. For example, if you were afraid of dogs, you could create an exposure hierarchy where you first look at a picture of a dog, then watch dog videos, then look at dogs from outside the fence of a dog park, then stand ten feet away from a leashed dog, and so on.

Creating an exposure hierarchy for your intruding historical pain points involves the same process. You'll outline exercises that you predict will evoke only minor emotional discomfort and work your way up to exposure exercises that you predict will bring on greater emotional discomfort. Sometimes it helps to picture the exposure hierarchy like a ladder, working from the lowest, most tolerable rung to the highest, most anxiety-provoking rung.

Let's begin. You can choose one historical pain point to focus on or include a variety of historical pain points, as you see fit. Tackling one at a time allows for more in-depth work; addressing a variety of historical pain points in your hierarchy is a more generalist approach. You'll want to come up with exposure exercises to evoke anxiety levels of 0 to 10. You can't be sure how much anxiety will arise for you at any given moment, so make your best prediction of the amount of distress that will come up for you—otherwise known as predicted *subjective units of distress* (SUDS). You can use Caroline's sample exposure hier- archy as a guide. A downloadable PDF and a blank hierarchy for you to complete can be found at www.newharbinger.com/50300.

Engaging in Your ERP Training Plan

Every time you engage in an exposure exercise outlined on your hierarchy, it is important to note your pre-exposure SUDS and your post-exposure SUDS (on a scale of 0 to 10). Again, SUDS refers to the amount of distress you are experiencing at the moment. How long does it take for your anxiety to subside? What else did you notice about your experience? Anything new or different than expected? By tracking and noting your results and your new learning, you allow your parent brain to witness how emotional discomfort is fleeting and passes on its own, once you stop struggling with it.

Exponential Progress

When we begin exposure-based work with our clients, they sometimes express concern about never-ending exposures because there are not enough hours in the day to address all of their historical pain points. But every time you work your exposure mental muscles, you rewire your brain to recognize its resilience and relinquish beliefs about your vulnerability and need to be protected from not-so-dangerous danger. These benefits grow exponentially with each additional exposure exercise

As you move through your exposure hierarchy, you will find that many items naturally drop off and no longer spark anxiety. We recommend checking each item to assess your emotional discomfort level. If it's low or nonexistent, there is no need to conduct any direct exposures with that pain point.

The exact exposures that work for you will differ from the exposures that are most effective for someone else struggling with the same historical pain point. However, the key ingredients of a high-quality exposure remain the same: repeatedly making full, open contact with the most anxiety-inducing aspects of an uncomfortable thought, feeling, or sensation without interruption or distraction. The more contact your brain has with feared stimuli, the more efficiently and effectively it learns to identify them as old news, not critical information about a current threat.

How Moving Past Historic Pain Points Rewires the Brain

You cannot erase your past, but you can become more self-aware and choose how to respond to your historic pain. By engaging in the parent brain rewiring exercises throughout this chapter, you have enhanced your ability to make sense of and move past these historical pain points. You can stop avoiding emotional distress and start living life on your terms. You recognize when your brain and body bring a past moment into your present, and you can choose how to respond. By giving conscious attention to your historical pain points, your brain integrates this fragmented information and no longer misinterprets past stressors as though they are unfolding now. You understand how emotional suffering is increased by fighting against the inevitable pain of being human. You know you can reduce emotional suffering by opening up and accepting uncomfortable feelings rather than fighting to deny them. With your brain's enhanced resilience, you are better equipped to move through future challenges and beyond.

CHAPTER 6

Finding Your Calm

David and Olivia's story offers a good illustration of this chapter's focus.

David is a dedicated, loving father whose parent brain has one noteworthy challenge area. Like many parents, David has trouble calming himself down in moments of frustration or concern about his children, Eden and Nate. He can be patient through countless parenting challenges, but when he notices his children being rude or disrespectful to others, it really sends him spiraling. Throughout his life, he has valued kindness and compassion for others, and he's strived to pass these on to his children. He's determined to raise well-mannered, polite children who are respectful, kind, and compassionate. When David and his wife, Olivia, began their parenting journey together, he felt confident that he would be able to shape their children into good human beings who would make the world a better place. Lately, though, he has been more frustrated and less confident in his ability to do so.

David's Parent Brain Default State: Overwhelmed + Reactive

A few weeks ago, David was driving his children to school when the pleasant drive turned disastrous, highlighting for David that it was time for him to improve his ability to calm himself down. As David drove, he listened to his children in the back seat talking about how "weird and annoying" another child at their school was. David jumped into their conversation: "We don't speak like that about others in this family." He glanced in the rearview mirror and could see Eden and Nate simultaneously roll their eyes and exchange glances at each other—a silent but clear signal of agreement that Dad was lame and clueless about how the real world operates. David took a deep breath and reminded himself of his job to raise kind, conscientious children. After a few more deep breaths, he attempted to engage them in a conversation about how bad it might feel if someone called them "weird and annoying." The kids stared out their windows and ignored him. David began to feel flooded and overwhelmed by the moment, and his emotional temperature went from 0 to 10.

He could feel his heart thumping in his chest and his face growing hot. His mind raced with thoughts about the ways he had failed to teach kindness to his children and the possible future implications of their lack of empathy as adults. His mind even went so far as to point out how weak and spineless he must be to have children who show so little respect for him. David was sure he had never disrespected his parents the way he's disrespected by his own kids. He tried to stuff down these uncomfortable thoughts and feelings, but it was all too much. David raised his voice and began directing an unhinged rant at his kids—empty threats about screen time restrictions and getting grounded—making it clear that they would not get to enjoy life until they learned the appropriate way to treat others.

What followed was all-around chaos and dysfunction. Eden and Nate began shouting back at David, calling him "mean" and saying from now on they only wanted to be driven by Mom. Nate even pointed out that if David wanted them to be nicer to other people, why was he being so mean to them? That one stung a little bit. And a light bulb went off for David. He knew he needed to find a better way to manage frustrating parenting moments. He wanted to connect with his children and instill his values in them, rather than losing his cool and triggering out-of-control battles.

Olivia's Parent Brain Default State: Striving for Calm + Groundedness

David's wife, Olivia, shares many of his values and also prioritizes raising children who are kind, respectful, and appreciative of the world around them. When Eden and Nate act in a way that Olivia feels is inappropriate, she also feels the tension and frustration boil up within her. Unlike David, though, Olivia has been working hard over the past few months to rewire her brain to effectively calm down, instead of becoming overwhelmed by negative thoughts and feelings. Calm, cool, collected parenting didn't exactly come naturally to Olivia, but she made it a priority to rewire her brain and shift her behavior.

Olivia has been working hard to enhance her ability to settle down her brain and body when she is triggered by a stressor, such as the kids misbehaving in the back seat. Of course, she is not perfect, and there are still times when she reacts first and thinks afterward. But overall, she has experienced an undeniable shift in the parenting climate—fewer moments of letting her emotions call the shots and more moments when she can press pause on her reaction and proceed with a more level, logical mindset. She has noticed that when she calms down she is better able to address situations with wisdom rather than reactivity.

For example, on Olivia's morning to drive the kids to school last week, the emotional climate in the car changed for no obvious reason. One moment Eden and Nate were goofing around together; nanoseconds later they were poking and kicking each other, each striving to come up with the best insult to bring the other to tears. This capped off a stressful, frustrating morning, and Olivia had very little bandwidth to tolerate this sibling battle. Every cell in Olivia's body urged her to pull over, get out of the car, and run from the chaos and noise. Instead, she opted to pull a few tools out of her Calm Yourself Down toolbox—acknowledging and validating the discomfort of the situation, practicing her breathing skills, and choosing an adaptive next step to help her move through the moment. In this moment she needed to calm down to continue safely driving the children to school. Thanks to her new coping tools, Olivia could let her wisdom-driven PFC take the driver's seat, rather than being at the mercy of her emotion-driven amygdala.

When it comes to your current ability to navigate stressful parenting moments, are you more like David or Olivia?

When you find yourself in a frustrating moment, does your emotion-driven amygdala or your wisdom-driven PFC take the driver's seat?

Do you have a readily available Calm Yourself Down toolbox to access when you are feeling out of control and unmoored?

If you do not yet have a customized Calm Yourself Down toolbox, fear not. This chapter is here to cocreate it with you. Once you have one, you will be better able to guide yourself and your family through the thrills and spills of parenting. Plus, there is no better way to teach your children the critical emotion regulation skill of being able to calm down their mind and body than by modeling it for them. It is one thing to tell them what to do, but it is so much more powerful to show them what to do.

A critical step in rewiring your brain to be less stressed and anxious is teaching it how to dial down its emotional overreaction to an unpleasant (but not dangerous) stressor. With a calm, cool, and collected mind within reach, you can swiftly move through a challenging moment, rather than getting stuck in it and feeling out of control.

This chapter will help you learn to:

- Regulate your emotional temperature

- Shift gears from amygdala-driven to PFC-driven moments

- More efficiently move from frustration and fear to calm and peace

- Model effective emotion regulation for your child

- Predict and proactively plan for emotionally triggering moments

Your Hardworking Amygdala

Why do some parents seem to move through frustrating moments with ease and grace while others seem to lose their cool so rapidly? No, it's not that some parents are just "better." Rather, some people have been born with a harder-working amygdala than others. If you self-identify as an anxious or highly sensitive person, chances are your amygdala is hyperaware of potential threats, which tend to flood your brain and leave you feeling overwhelmed and sometimes unable to calm down. When your PFC receives an overload of information from your amygdala, it operates less efficiently as it attempts to process and make sense of the flood. If you find it difficult to think clearly when you are emotionally triggered, it's not just you; it is difficult for *anyone* to think clearly once their amygdala has sounded the danger alarm. Sometimes in these moments, our brain feels like a computer with too many windows or applications operating. For any information-processing mechanism, including your brain, trying to process so much information all at once tends to backfire and actually slows things down. And as we all have experienced, when a system gets overloaded and jammed, a reboot is often necessary.

Emotion Regulation for Two

You're not the only one who will benefit from the investment of time and energy you are putting into learning how to calm down your mind and body. Your child also has much to gain. Thanks to the mirror neurons at play between you and your child (no matter how old they are), when they witness you down-regulating and cooling your emotional temperature, their brain too will rewire itself to more effectively calm down and self-regulate. Your ability to regulate your own emotions can simultaneously assist your child in learning how to feel calm, safe, and in control.

Sometimes parents find themselves in an emotional distress feedback loop with their child, feeding off of each other's activated emotional states, both unable to calm down in the moment. You can break this feedback loop by practicing calming yourself down in the presence of your emotionally activated child. As they observe you flexing your self-regulation muscles, their brain will actually begin to mimic yours. Rather than yelling or acting before thinking, you take a series of slow, gentle breaths and then choose how to proceed in a stressful moment, and their brains will mimic these same operating instructions.

Perhaps up to now you've experienced only the flip side of this brain-based relationship between you and your child. When your child witnesses you at the mercy of your emotions, they will also feel out of control. Their brain will learn that their emotions are in charge and calling the shots. If their feelings tell them to yell, they must yell—if their feelings tell them to throw their toy, then they must throw their toy. But by practicing and modeling your own emotion regulation skills, your child now can learn that their big feelings don't have to control them in the moment.

Calming Down Your Amygdala

All humans learn different ways of managing emotions throughout their lives. Take a moment to think about how your own life experience has taught you to calm down in moments of high stress, frustration, or anxiety, leading to ineffective coping strategies like these:

- Discharging emotions on the person who is triggering you (such as yelling, fighting, being passive-aggressive)

- Avoiding the topic or situation that is triggering heightened emotions (such as repressing feelings, ignoring the situation at hand, shutting down)

Although common, these strategies are sadly ineffective. As you're learning, there are other ways of managing stress, frustration, and anxiety to truly calm down your parent brain and promote more grounded, effective ways of living and parenting. This chapter will give you evidence-based tools (meaning they actually work) to help you hack into your nervous system and shift from an amygdala-driven moment to a PFC-driven moment more rapidly and effectively.

The Body Under Stress

When a stressful event occurs, the amygdala sends a distress signal to the hypothalamus. To recap, the hypothalamus functions like a command center to regulate important bodily functions, including thirst, hunger, mood, libido, sleep, and body temperature. After the hypothalamus receives a warning message from the amygdala, it activates the sympathetic nervous system by sending signals through the autonomic nerves to the adrenal glands, which respond by pumping the hormone epinephrine (also known as adrenaline) into the bloodstream. The body then responds to this surge of adrenaline with various physiological changes, which together make up the fight-flight-freeze response.

Physiological Changes of the Fight-Flight-Freeze Response

When the fight-flight-freeze response is triggered, the human body undergoes a whole host of physiological changes to prepare to face the threat at hand and attempt to survive. From an evolutionary standpoint, these physiological changes are logical and reasonable—we would not have survived this long as a species without the fight-flight-freeze response. However, when the amygdala experiences a false alarm, these physiological changes create highly uncomfortable body sensations. These sensations are commonly associated with stress, anxiety, and panic. As you read through this list, consider whether this evolutionarily advantageous process may be the cause of the discomfort you (and so many others) feel when stressed or anxious.

- **Increased breathing rate → extra oxygen sent to the brain to increase alertness**

  Shallow, rapid breathing, hyperventilation, feeling like you're suffocating or not getting enough oxygen, difficulty thinking or concentrating, foggy headed, feeling "out of it"

- **Increased heart rate → allows more nutrients to reach your large muscle groups (arms, legs, torso)**

  Racing or pounding heart, tightness in chest, feeling like something is wrong with your body

- **Increased sweating → cools the body down to avoid overheating**

  Feeling sweaty or clammy

- **Dilated pupils → allows for more light and enhanced visual detection of threats**

Blurred or distorted vision, experience of being hyperaware or overly attuned to stimuli

- **Muscle contraction → protects vital organs from injury or pain, similar to an internal shield**

  Tension, tightness throughout the body, muscle aches and pains

- **Shift of blood flow (from small muscle groups toward large muscle groups) → extra glucose-enriched blood is redirected to the arms and legs to promote actions necessary in fight-flight-freeze mode**

  Feeling shaky, jittery, unsettled, face pale or flushed, hands and feet cold and tingly

- **Shift of blood flow (from gut toward large muscle groups) → extra glucose-enriched blood is redirected to the arms and legs to promote actions necessary in fight-flight-freeze mode**

  Upset stomach, feelings of nausea, gastrointestinal distress including diarrhea or vomiting

When the amygdala determines there is no immediate threat to be managed after all, it signals the hypothalamus to shift gears and turn on the parasympathetic nervous system, which conserves energy and down-regulates bodily functions when the coast is clear. When your parasympathetic nervous system is in charge of your physiology, your heart rate, blood pressure, and breathing rate slow, blood flow redirects to your gut and other smaller muscle groups (such as your hands and feet), and you return to a state often known as rest-and-digest. Your sympathetic and parasympathetic nervous systems together act like the gas and brakes on a car. Your sympathetic system is the gas that revs you up, and your parasympathetic system is the brakes that slow you down.

Your Body Under Stress

Although the human body comes with a fight-flight-freeze response prein-stalled (when it comes to survival, customizations and special requests are never a good idea), there are nuances to how each person experiences their body under stress. For example, when David is feeling triggered, he tends to first notice a heavy feeling in his chest; moments later comes a hot, sweaty feeling in his face. When Olivia is feeling worked up, she first notices that she is having a hard time thinking clearly and gathering her thoughts. She then starts feeling out of control and detached from the world around her. Both David and Olivia experience the same fight-flight-freeze response, set in motion by their hardworking amygdalae, relayed through their hypothalamus, and put into full motion by their adrenaline-doused bodies. But each has a unique phys-iology and different life experiences and therefore will experience unique acti-vation of their sympathetic nervous system.

Parent Brain Rewiring Exercise: Your Fight-Flight-Freeze Experience

Take a few moments to reflect on the fight-flight-freeze sensations you are most aware of when you are operating under stress. Consider the following questions and note your responses in your Training Journal.

1. Which of these sensations do you associate with your mind and body under stress?

   - Feelings of suffocation or difficulty breathing
   - Rapid heart rate
   - Tightness in chest
   - Upset stomach or nausea
   - Tingly cold hands and/or feet
   - Increased sweating
   - Feeling dizzy
   - Difficulty concentrating or thinking clearly

- Blurred or altered vision

- Feeling shaky

- Feeling out of control

2. How uncomfortable do you find these sensations? Rate each sensation on a scale of 0 to 10, with 0 being no discomfort and 10 being the most uncomfortable.

3. How do you interpret these sensations? Are there any noteworthy thoughts that tend to surface when you are experiencing these sensations? Look for catastrophic thinking patterns.

 4. Where in your body do you feel your stress response the most? Take a moment to sketch out your body under stress in your Training Journal.

Here is David's example:

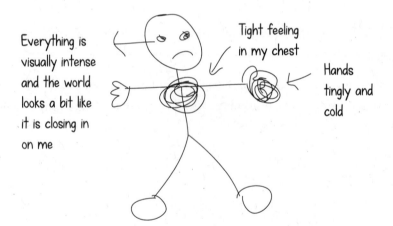

Activating Your Rest-and-Digest Response

At this point, we imagine you're more familiar with your body's fight-flight-freeze response than you are with its counterbalancing rest-and-digest response. This chapter provides you with tools, via your autonomic nervous system and associated physiological responses, and exercises to shift your body's response from sympathetic to parasympathetic when there is no active threat to address.

As you have been practicing in chapter 3, you can inform your amygdala there is no danger by rewiring your PFC to more readily shift from catastrophic to realistic thinking mode. Consider this use of the mind to calm down the rest of the body a *mind-down* approach to regulating your emotional temperature— informing your amygdala that you are currently safe and sound. Once your amygdala has received the all-clear message, your PFC can take over and initi- ate effective problem solving to guide you and your children through stressful parenting moments.

Proceed with Caution

In the first few sessions of anxiety treatment, we always ask clients what strate- gies they've already tried to manage their symptoms. We commonly hear "I tried relaxation exercises like deep breathing and meditation, but they didn't work." In fact, they often report these efforts left them feeling more stressed and anxious. Trying too hard to elicit a state of calm can backfire. When you feel desperate to relax and terrified of feeling anxious, the pressure to calm down is much too high; no wonder so many only feel more stressed.

If you can adopt an open, flexible attitude regarding your anxious thoughts and feelings and tell yourself *I'd like to calm down, but I'm not in danger if I don't (or can't)*, you're one step closer to activating your parasympathetic nervous system's rest-and-digest response. So keep in mind, as you move through the exercises in this chapter, you are *choosing* to calm down. It is not that you *must* calm down or else something terrible will happen to you. It just happens to be more comfortable and less energy-intensive to hang out in a state of rest-and- digest when there is no active danger to manage. You are safe and okay, whether your body is revved up with stress or 'chillaxing,' as the kids would say. It is not dangerous to be anxious or stressed, but it does make the moment less fun and enjoyable.

Slow Breathing: The Volume Dial for Your Emotions

The most powerful and readily accessible tool you have to reassure your amygdala there is no threat is your breath. Just five minutes of slow breathing can make a difference. By breathing more slowly and steadily, with less intensity, you can activate your parasympathetic nervous system and send a signal to your amygdala: *We're not in danger, so there's no reason to breathe so rapidly and fuel up with all this extra oxygen. There's no need to run and no one to fight, so less oxygen is required to manage this moment. Slow, gentle breaths are all we need.*

Some people find that their brains quickly wander to different topics, or that the very act of focusing on the breath makes them so hyperaware that their breathing becomes forced and tight. You have already begun rewiring your brain to be more mindful, thanks to those exercises you completed in chapter 4. You understand how to harness your attention and redirect it back to the anchor you selected for the mindful moment you are engaging in. For these breathing exercises, your breath is the anchor. Every time you notice your mind wandering off, with thoughts such as *This is not working* or *Am I doing this right?* or any other thoughts, you need only to acknowledge the thought and then gently return your attention to your breath. You don't need to argue with these thoughts, make them go away, or engage with them any more than by simply noticing when they surface.

Parent Brain Rewiring Exercise: Slow Breathe Past Anxious Moments

Part A: For the next week, practice slow breathing twice a day for five minutes, once in the morning and once in the evening. It helps to set a timer so you don't have to watch a clock.

1. Find a quiet place where you can focus your attention on your breath.

2. Rest your hand gently on your stomach and slowly breathe in for three seconds. As your hand rises, slowly count 1...2...3. Picture the air rising through your body, from your belly upward toward your brain, filling your brain with a fresh dose of oxygen.

3. Gently hold your breath for three seconds, 1...2...3.

4. Slowly breathe out for three seconds, 1...2...3. Notice your hand on your stomach falling. Purse your lips gently as you slowly release air. Picture the oxygen moving slowly from the top of your head, slowly making its way down through your body to the soles of your feet.

5. Gently hold your breath for three seconds, 1...2...3.

6. Repeat.

Some people find it helpful to ground themselves with a visual cue. Feel free to use the image here to guide your breathing and keep yourself grounded during this exercise. It may be helpful to gently rest your finger on each square as you move through the exercise, holding for three seconds on a square and then moving to the next. Repeat until the five-minute timer sounds.

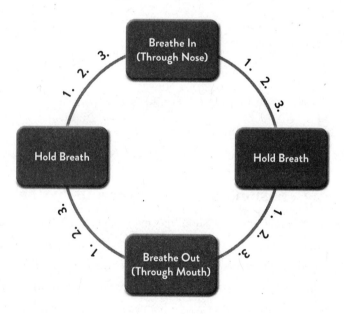

Now take out your Training Journal and reflect on your experience. How did you feel before, during, and after this exercise? Write down anything you noticed.

Part B: Now to take this slow breathing tool on the road. Use slow breathing anywhere, whenever you begin to feel stress, anxiety, or frustration arising in your body. It's your first line of defense for an amygdala misfiring during stress-ful parenting moments.

For the next week, track your experience with using your new breathing tool to move through stressful parenting moments. Each time you experience one, record a description of the situation, your initial reaction, and your distress level rating. After taking five minutes to slow breathe, update your distress level rating. What do you notice?

You can use your Training Journal or download a blank Slow Breathing Log PDF at www.newharbinger.com/50300, where you'll also find David's log example.

As you track your experience, record the following information (in your Training Journal or on the blank chart PDF):

- Date/Time:

- Situation:

- Initial reaction:

- Pre-slow breathing distress level (0–10):

- Post-slow breathing distress level (0–10):

- How you chose to handle the stressful moment:

Releasing Tension from Your Nervous System

When your amygdala senses you're in danger, it signals your hypothalamus to activate your sympathetic nervous system. As we've discussed, the muscles throughout your body contract and tighten to protect your vital organs, such as your heart, lungs, and kidneys, from external threats. But the opposite is also true. When your amygdala determines that you're safe, it signals for your hypothalamus to activate your parasympathetic nervous system, which initiates a release of the tension held by your contracted muscles. When your brain realizes that you're choosing to forgo your armor of tense muscles, it knows it's a safe moment to relax and soak up some well-deserved rest-and-digest time.

These safety/danger signals travel both ways. Tensed muscles signal your amygdala that you're in danger. Relaxing your muscles signals your amygdala that the coast is clear. This two-way information exchange enables you to activate your parasympathetic nervous system on demand by relaxing your muscles in a repetitive, systematic, and intentional fashion with progressive muscle relaxation (PMR).

Progressive Muscle Relaxation (PMR): The Pressure Valve for Your Nervous System

You've learned to use slow breathing to initiate a shift from a fight-flight-freeze to a rest-and-digest managed moment. PMR is another simple exercise that calms down your mind and body. PMR involves practicing tensing and relaxing all your muscles in an exaggerated way. If you have been experiencing anxiety for a while, your body is likely familiar with holding tension for extended periods of time and needs some training on how to shift gears and release the tension. By practicing releasing the tension systematically, your amygdala will note how your body feels safe enough to be open, loose, and relaxed, thus signaling no immediate danger and no need to be in fight-flight-freeze mode.

Parent Brain Rewiring Exercise: PMR in Practice

Part A: Tense and Release

1. Find a comfortable place like a chair or bed to sit or lie down.

2. Mindfully and intentionally tense all the muscles in your body. Tense your fists, your arms, your face, forehead, eyes, and mouth. Tense your shoulders and feel them rise. Tense your stomach, your buttocks and thighs, your calves. Tense your toes and notice them curl. Hold this tension for fifteen full seconds.

3. Next, practice releasing this tension. Visualize a rag doll or an overcooked piece of spaghetti. Feel the weight of your body parts as the tension releases and you sink into the bed or chair beneath you. Take a moment to roll your head around a bit, stretch out your mouth, or

shake out your hands. Imagine releasing the tension that was once held tightly in your body out into the world.

4. Repeat three more times.

Part B: Developing Your PMR Muscle Memory

To promote your PMR muscle memory, practice PMR for two minutes twice a day for the next week, once in the morning and once before bed. Track your experience using your Training Journal. We recommend tracking:

- Day/Time:

- Pre-PMR stress level (0–10):

- Post-PMR stress level (0–10):

- Any additional notes:

Here's a sample from Olivia's log:

- Day/Time: 2/15 in a.m.

- Pre-PMR stress level (0–10): 6/10

- Post-PMR stress level (0–10): 4/10

- Any additional notes: Woke up feeling anxious for the long, jam-packed day ahead. Didn't realize how much tension I was holding even before getting out of bed.

PMR in the Real World

Once you have had some practice applying PMR when you are feeling relatively calm and settled, you are ready to use PMR in real, stressful parenting moments. Imagine you are running late trying to get the kids out the door for school, and as you are herding them out to the car, your child remembers they need to bring their musical instrument and haven't even filled out the week's practice log yet. At this moment, you have two options. You can:

1. Snap at your child and tell them they should've been more prepared, threatening to leave without their instrument and practice log the

next time this happens. Maybe some natural consequences will teach them to be more organized, right?!

2. Pause for a beat. Take a moment to do one round (fifteen-ish seconds) of PMR to release a little of that tension building in your body and gather your thoughts. Then calmly tell your child to run upstairs and grab what they need while you wait in the car.

If you go with option 1, will you get to school or work any faster? When you yell or express unhinged frustration with your child, do they move more efficiently? Or have you noticed an opposite pattern? Does your child get overwhelmed or defensive in response to your frustrated outburst? Often the overflow of raw emotions when we express frustration with our children actually slows down an already backed-up process. By taking a few moments to engage in some PMR on the fly, you will actually save yourself time and decrease the discomfort associated with a stressful parenting moment such as this one.

Parent Brain Rewiring Exercise: PMR on the Fly

For the next week, every time you are in a high-stress situation, engage in one round of PMR. If you have a few extra moments, we recommend treating yourself to three rounds of PMR to further help your nervous system down-regulate. Keep a record of your on-the-fly PMR practice (as soon as you get the chance), just as you did in the previous exercise. Use your Training Journal to track:

- Day/Time:

- Stressful parenting moment/situation:

- Pre-PMR stress level (0–10):

- Post-PMR stress level (0–10):

- Any additional notes:

Here's an example from Olivia's log:

- Day/Time: 2/24, 4:50 p.m.

- Stressful parenting moment/situation: Dropping Eden off at dance class and realized I was supposed to bring her in her full costume for a dress rehearsal. I could sense her embarrassment, and mine too for that matter.

- Pre-PMR stress level (0–10): 7/10

- Post-PMR stress level (0–10): 4/10

- Any additional notes: Felt really good to ground myself so I felt able to get a game plan and figure out some logical next steps to manage the moment.

How These Exercises Rewire Your Parent Brain for Less Stress and Anxiety

By practicing slowing your breathing and relaxing your muscles, you're signaling to your amygdala that you're safe and sound. From there, your amygdala can signal the hypothalamus to shift gears from a fight-flight-freeze response to a rest-and-digest response.

Change Your Mind's Channel

Sometimes you are going to feel so flooded with stress and anxiety that gathering the emotional resources for slow breathing or PMR may feel unrealistic. That's okay—we get it! Just like working toward physical fitness goals, your energy and ability to engage in certain brain rewiring exercises may vary. No matter where you are on any given day, you are taking meaningful steps toward becoming a calmer, more grounded parent. That is impressive in and of itself. Sure, it might sound nice to always approach parenting challenges with the wisdom and steady presence of the Dalai Lama, but there will still be moments when the best you can muster is the impulse control of *Seinfeld*'s George Costanza (for readers unfamiliar with this character, picture a grown man with the emotional range of a toddler).

It is true that the only way past difficult emotions is through them, but there is a time and place for everything, and sometimes the healthiest way to move past an emotionally challenging moment is to take a pause rather than plowing through. Moments of emotional overwhelm are never the time to make big decisions or take life-altering actions, as the thoughts that bubble up in these moments are often extreme and inaccurate. Instead of reactively plowing through these moments, try pressing pause. After a brief time-out, you can work to move through the situation, changing the channel with a calm, grounded state of mind.

The trick in these times is to focus your attention on anything in the outside world besides your own extreme thoughts and feelings. It could be the sky, a chair, your dog, or even a speck of lint if that's what you've got to work with. It doesn't matter what you focus on, as long as you guide your attention away from your extreme thoughts and feelings. And remember, you are redirecting your attention not because your thoughts and feelings are dangerous, but because you'd rather not feel controlled by them at that moment. Think of the difference between choosing to go for a run and running in terror from an attacker. Even though you are engaging in the same physical action, your amygdala knows whether you are running for chosen, valued exercise, rather than to avoid something dangerous.

If your amygdala thinks you are focusing on external stimuli to escape from your out-of-control thoughts and feelings, it will signal your hypothalamus for your fight-flight-freeze response. For example, if David turns up the volume on the car speakers because he *can't handle hearing one more second of the kids fighting*, his brain understands him to be running from something dangerous rather than engaging in something valued. If instead he plays his music and tells himself, *I deserve to hear the sound of my favorite band. I may not be able to control their bickering, but I can control what I do with myself at this moment*, his amygdala will interpret the act of playing music as neutral and nothing to be alarmed about.

Redirecting your attention away from the uncomfortable thoughts and feelings of a stressful parenting moment and toward a rich sensory experience gives your mind and body a well-deserved moment to reboot and recalibrate. From there, you will have an easier time calming yourself down and *choosing* how to proceed.

The 3-3-3 Grounding Tool

Begin by bringing you awareness to the present moment. Notice your feet making contact with the earth beneath you. Then notice your legs and lower body—whether seated, lying down, or standing tall. Notice the weight of your arms resting by your sides. Next, take a look at the space around you.

1. Name three things you can **see**. For example, *I see my dog in her bed, blue sky outside the window, and a blanket draped over the couch.*

2. Name three things you can **touch**. For example, *I feel the soft sleeve of my sweatshirt partially covering my hands, the carpet under my bare feet, and my fingertips making contact with the smooth, warm metal of my computer.*

3. Name three things you can **hear**. For example, *I hear my dog's collar jingling as she scratches her ear, the sound of the air moving through the vents, and a car driving by outside.*

Now that you have the basic idea, try the whole 3-3-3 grounding exercise for yourself. In this moment, notice three things you can see, three things you can touch, and three things you can hear. You can say them out loud, or if you're in a public space, just say them in your head. You can repeat this exercise as many times as you need; many of our clients find that doing it just once helps them deescalate spiraling thoughts and emotions.

Changing Your Sensory Experience

You can change your mental channel by surprising your brain with a new, pleasant, and/or unexpected sensory experience. The goal of the following sensory-based exercises is to get your brain engaged in the current moment via your senses, so it can take a pause from tending to an extreme (and disproportionate) emotional reaction. The listed items are suggestions; feel free to try other options.

Change What You *Taste*

- Carry mints or gum for an on-the-go sensory experience.

- Drink something soothing or refreshing (sparkling water, hot tea, lemonade).

- Check the fridge and sample a little something you have not had in a while (pickles, salad dressing, chocolate sauce).

Change What You *Smell*

- Carry lavender oil or another favorite scent to inhale.

- Use a lip balm with an appealing smell.

- Keep lotion in your favorite scent handy.

Change What You *Hear*

- Create a "Change My Mind's Channel" playlist.

- Listen to a song you know by heart so you can sing along and really engage with it.

- Tune in to a new sound around you and think about the last time (if ever) you really listened to it (street traffic, drippy faucet, refrigerator hum).

Change What You *Feel*

- Pet your dog or cat (or another pet) or a soft, comforting textured cloth.

- Apply lotion and notice how your skin changes from feeling dry to feeling nourished.

- Play with Silly Putty, slime, or some other fidget toy (if you're like many of our parent clients, you've likely got something like this lying around at home).

Change Your *Body Position*

- If you find yourself pacing, sit down.

- If you feel trapped in your body, do some jumping jacks or run the steps in a stairwell.

- If you are clenching your fists, open up your hands and really extend your fingers.

- If your shoulders are raised, slowly let them ease down to a more relaxed position.

- If your arms are crossed or tight to your sides or chest, slowly extend them out to the side or above your head.

Parent Brain Rewiring Exercise: Draw Your Attention to Paper

Time to get your creative juices flowing. For this exercise you will need a piece of paper and a pen or pencil.

Begin by focusing your attention on an object in the room. Start free-drawing it, trying to not spend any time planning it out or trying to get it "right." All that matters is mindfully paying attention to all aspects of the object: curves, lines, pattern, texture, shape. Work that mindfulness muscle and resist the urge to judge your drawing as "good" or "bad."

Observe what it feels like to draw. How much pressure are you applying to your drawing utensil? What does it feel like to press it into the paper? When was the last time you allowed yourself a moment to do something like this?

Work Your Emotion Regulation Muscles Daily

With these emotional regulation strategies in mind, identify one mildly frustrating but necessary daily task. Before you complete the task, decide which strategy you will use if you notice your sympathetic nervous system is running the show, causing you to feel a disproportionate stress reaction. Use one or a combination of these strategies until you feel less consumed by "hot" thoughts or feelings. The possibilities are endless, and you're welcome to add your own ideas.

Use your Training Journal to log your experience and reflect on what it feels like to employ these emotion regulation strategies in the moment. Was your distress higher or lower after using the strategy? Do you notice any patterns? Are there some challenges that are easier to down-regulate than others?

Here's a sample from David's log:

- Date: 3/11

- Stressful task: Taking a work call from the pick-up car line at the kids' school

- Emotion regulation strategy used: 3-3-3 grounding tool

- Notes/Observations: Was feeling jittery and cloudy headed before the call. After using 3-3-3 grounding tool, I felt more able to focus on my upcoming call rather than getting lost in anxious thoughts about my inability to multitask.

Some parents we work with find it helpful to create notes in their phones listing their top three emotion regulation strategies—like speed bumps to help them slow down. The main challenge with using the strategies you've learned is that moments of high emotion arise suddenly. When your amygdala is running the show, it may not feel like you have the time or clarity to access your emotional brakes. Regular practice with these exercises can help you do just that and better dial down intense emotions and uncomfortable physical sensations.

How These Exercises Rewire Your Parent Brain to Reduce Stress and Anxiety

When every cell in your body is revved up and ready to fight-flight-freeze, switching gears and activating your parasympathetic nervous system's rest-and-digest response is challenging but not impossible. By learning how to turn down the volume on unnecessarily intense emotions, you can proceed with a cooler mindset, no longer at the mercy of your emotional reactions.

The exercises throughout this chapter are so powerful because they serve to ground you in your physical senses. By shifting your attention to your present sensory experience, you give your brain some space from your amygdala's alarm signals and the unhelpful thoughts that keep you stuck in your intense emotions.

The next time you find yourself in a stressful parenting moment, give yourself the gift of one or more of these emotion regulation exercises. You'll find that your body and mind calm down after a brief time-out and you can then choose how to efficiently proceed through the stressful situation.

CHAPTER 7

Relinquishing Control

This chapter's story relates what Ali learned from how his sister, Zariah, handled a seemingly inevitable challenge: the parent-child power struggle.

Ali thrives with order and control. Not that he views himself as overly controlling; he just has always strived to set himself (and others) up for success by carefully planning for all mitigating factors and trying to leave as little to chance as possible. He prides himself on always being conscientious and careful, and his fastidious nature has paid off generously in academic and professional success. When Ali started on his parenting journey, he felt confident these same values would serve him well in this new role of father.

Ali and his younger sister, Zariah, were very close, even more so since their mother passed away when they were only in high school. They leaned on one another in times of need and called the other one out when they deserved it. Now they lived just a few streets away from each other with their own families. Zariah and Ali bonded over their love for cooking and eating, and they held similar beliefs about ambition. Both knew that life wasn't fair or easy, so they each felt determined to "be the change" and create the life they hoped to live. They had worked hard to reap the rewards in their lives, both personally and professionally.

Zariah's son, Emmett, and Ali's son, Lucas, were two years apart and shared a special bond as cousins. They grew up playing together at many family gatherings. At these family get-togethers, it was apparent that Ali and Zariah had different approaches to parenting. Ali, knowing that order and control had often led him to success, attempted to instill the same method in his parenting. He believed that a good parent does not give in to their child's whims and momentary demands but instead establishes rules and expectations for how their child should live their life. Ali felt it his duty as a father to minimize his son's contact with risks and unhealthy influences that might lead to costly consequences. After all, he wanted only the best for his son.

One January a huge snowstorm came through overnight. The next day the boys' school called a snow day and canceled classes. The boys were giddy with joy knowing that they could stay home all day, watch TV, and play in the mountains of fresh snow. Zariah and Ali also couldn't get to work because of the snow, so they decided to work from home together so the boys could entertain themselves during the day. When Ali told Lucas, age six, that his aunt and cousin were coming over, he exclaimed, "Best day ever!" Ali loved to see how much Lucas cherished his relationships with his aunt and cousin. Soon after, Zariah and Emmett, age eight, arrived, and the adults headed to Ali's home office (kitchen) to try to get some work done. The kids headed off, talking over each other in delight, reviewing all of their plans for this unexpected day of school-free fun.

A few hours later, the boys barged into the kitchen where Zariah and Ali were working and pleaded with their parents to let them play out in the snow. Zariah was in the middle of a conference call, so Ali agreed to help the boys suit up.

Ali took out Lucas's snow pants, coat, hat, and gloves. Lucas started complaining that he didn't want to wear his snow pants. At first, Ali ignored his son's objections and continued to dress him. But Lucas only objected even louder. Ali sighed with frustration and thought Here we go again... Why can't he just listen to me? As these thoughts cued up, he automatically snapped: "You are wearing your snow pants or you can't play outside. End of story!" But of course it was not the end. Lucas began to bargain with Ali: "Please, Dad, I don't want to wear snow pants. They are itchy and uncomfortable. Plus, Emmett isn't wearing his snow pants." Ali then tried to get his nephew to put on his snow pants. Now he met resistance from both boys, who began to tear up as they whined with frustration.

Zariah came in to see what was going on. She tried her best to defuse the power struggle. She told the boys that even though she and Ali wanted them to wear snow pants so they could play outside for longer in comfort, at the end of the day it was their bodies, and they could make the final decision. The boys sighed with relief, and their excitement instantly returned.

Ali could see that Zariah's strategy of letting the boys have the final say relieved the conflict, yet he still was stuck on the fact that the boys would get wet and cold outside. Zariah said she was sure they would learn from these natural consequences. If they were too cold, they would likely have to cut short their fun and come inside. Maybe then they would put on their snow pants, or maybe they would be done playing outside—she trusted that the boys would make a choice that worked for them. The point was taken by Ali, but he still felt like the score was now Parents: 0, Kids: 1.

Zariah shared another perspective: She could see how it felt that way, but she reminded Ali that by choosing to disengage from the power struggle with Lucas, he could free up his emotional energy to be used more effectively toward achieving his ultimate goal. In this case, Ali was trying to protect Lucas and keep him safe, but was there another way to accomplish this besides fighting with him? Maybe, in a calmer moment, they could discuss how the body reacts to cold temperatures and how keeping the body dry and warm allows you to tolerate being outside longer. Perhaps he could take Lucas sledding; he could gear up in his own snow pants and let Lucas decide whether to wear his snow pants. But maybe he could keep Lucas's snow pants handy, and if Lucas complained about being wet and cold, he could lovingly offer them to his son. Zariah explained to Ali that allowing a child to have more control over certain spheres of their life does not mean you stop trying to find innovative ways to keep them healthy and happy, but it does mean having more tools in your toolbox besides control-based strategies. The parent isn't giving in or giving up; rather, they can zoom out and see that they are no longer being effective with their child; it's time to try a different approach.

Ali's Parent Brain Default State: Control at All Costs

Ali was exhausted and frustrated. He felt like he was running in a hamster wheel—the harder he tried to get Lucas to listen and obey him, the more hopeless he felt about his ability to parent effectively. He was stuck: If he gave in to the boys, he would feel like a bad father/uncle, too lazy and ineffective to make the boys do the right thing. If he held his ground and did not let the boys play in the snow unless they wore snow pants, this would likely lead to more time wasted, plenty of tears, and a day of fun changed to a day of tension and emotional distress. This parenting moment (and, if he was being honest with himself, many others) felt like a lose-lose situation. He knew his current approach was clearly not working, but he just couldn't see another way.

He started questioning his parenting skills. Was he doing something wrong? Was his son just more stubborn than his nephew? While Emmett seemed to usually go with the flow, Ali felt like Lucas objected to his every request. He had always judged his sister as not being a tough enough parent, too often letting her son call the shots. He often chided her for this. He felt she was just being lazy or avoidant, not realizing there was an intention in her allowing Emmett to sometimes learn through his own choices.

Zariah's Parent Brain Default State: Flexible Parenting Control

Zariah claimed to have the same parenting goals as Ali. She too considered it her top life priority to provide her son with the key building blocks to become a competent, kind, successful man. Zariah's brain operated within the limits of what she could control while using other tools, beyond brute force, to gently guide her son.

As much as Zariah preferred that her son stay dry and warm while playing in the snow, she could see the snow pants struggle unfolding and decided to take action by accepting the limits of her control. Back when Emmett was a baby, if she had decided he needed protection from the winter elements and dressed him in a snowsuit, he could not undo her decision. But now that Emmett was eight, he certainly could dress and undress himself based on his preferences. Plus, she believed (with a few exceptions) that he was old enough to experience the natural consequences of making misguided choices for weather-appropriate clothing.

She knew if she yelled long enough and loud enough she could get him to put on her choice of clothing, but yelling didn't align with her parenting values. Arguing until Emmett complied would only drain her emotionally and spoil the boys' excitement, making the day a big disappointment for all. She wanted to preserve her energy for her work day so she could later relax and have fun with the kids.

Like Ali, Zariah often encountered resistance to her parental requests. It helped to remind herself that it was natural and age appropriate for an eight-year-old to test limits. She followed the philosophy of choosing her battles. In some situations Emmett would have to comply, no matter how upset he became. For example, when it came to applying sunblock on hot summer days, her word was law; he was way too young to understand the consequences of sunburns and the correlation between sun exposure and skin cancer. It was her job as the mom to understand this; when he was old enough to understand, she'd explain it, and when he was old enough to decide for himself, she hoped he'd remember.

In other scenarios, such as this snow pants struggle, Zariah opted to give up the tug-of-war with her son. She let him "win" control over certain moments and allowed him to expand his sense of autonomy and responsibility for his health and safety. Letting go of control in certain situations was in line with her long-term parenting goals. She could see over time that her son's confidence and intrinsic motivation to make good choices aligned with her goal of having him lead a joy-filled, meaningful life. Whenever Zariah convinced herself to intentionally relinquish control to Emmett, she became more confident in his ability to manage what life had in store for him, occasional obstacles and all. She tolerated the uncertainty and discomfort of letting go in order to let him practice making age-appropriate choices on his journey toward self-reliance. Until then, she would serve as his trusted life copilot, taking the controls when necessary and appropriate, and enjoying the flight together.

As Zariah understands—and Ali is beginning to—rewiring your brain to accept the limits of your control not only helps you decrease your overall parenting stress level and preserve more energy for other aspects of life that bring you joy, but it also greatly benefits your child. By disengaging from power struggles and allowing your child additional opportunities to choose how to proceed (in select age-appropriate ways) you give them the gift of fortitude and hardiness. Using these important behavioral experiments, they will learn through experience which choices lead them to success and which to negative outcomes—whether that be cold, soggy pants or a lower grade for a late assignment. When your child confronts the results of their choices, in measured and surmountable ways, you are helping them rewire their brain to be more effective and competent. There is no better teacher than your child's firsthand experience to offer guidance on how to obtain a more desirable outcome the next time they find themselves in a similar situation.

This chapter will help you learn to:

- Understand the benefits to letting go of control

- Recognize your amygdala's automatic reactions, desperate for controlled outcomes

- Move toward feelings of empowered acceptance, rather than defeat and complacency

- Work through inevitable power struggles in a balanced and effective way

- Enhance the quality of your relationship with your child, while supporting their developing sense of self

The Inevitability of Parent-Child Power Struggles

Power struggles are a parenting rite of passage that happen over and over again. The key is to not be surprised or disappointed each time one occurs. It is developmentally appropriate for children to test limits and boundaries as they explore newfound autonomy and reasoning skills with each developmental milestone. For example, school-age children may choose which friends they want to play with; a tween may decide how to spend their hard-earned money; a teenager can choose their after-school activities. Validating their decisions, even if they did not engage in *your* preferred choice, builds their confidence and trust in their decision-making abilities. This helps them feel competent and supported by you at any age. They will be more likely to come to you for support and guidance as they continue to encounter challenges.

You also want to consider what appropriate control looks like in your own culture and community. There is no perfect or right way to parent. However, you can find a healthy balance that works for you and your family. You can find a parenting style that incorporates your values as a parent and an individual. And finding balance in your parenting style will allow for more of those positive, meaningful parent-child connections.

Parent Brain Rewiring Exercise: Tracking Your Power Struggles

Take a moment to reflect on common parenting power struggles for you and your child. Note in your Training Journal:

- Are there any recurring themes or triggers? Common struggles include: food, picking out clothing, friends, schoolwork, and respect.

- How many power struggles occur in a week?

- What is the level of emotional distress (0 to 10) they cause?

  - For you

  - For your child

  - For the entire family

- How do your parenting control behaviors backfire?

- If you let go of control, what do you fear might happen? What is the likelihood of those negative outcomes? Does parent guilt show up when you choose to let go?

- What alternative behavior could you engage in with your child instead of grasping for control?

It is also important to know your child and their temperament. What makes them a unique child to parent? Not all siblings are created equal. Some will be more compliant with parenting efforts, but overly controlling them may lead children to internal self-doubt, making it difficult for them to learn to trust their own inner wisdom. Others may be more strong-willed and react with opposition to your control efforts. If your child has ADHD or lagging executive functioning skills, they may require more order and structure to reach their potential. If your child has anxiety, they may require more compassion and nudges of encouragement to engage and thrive in settings outside the home.

Take note of your own control qualities. What is your need for control like? Has that changed at all since becoming a parent? You may recognize that you need to step back and control less. Alternatively, you may need to step up and provide more structure.

Are You Really Winning with Control?

If you could control all of the outcomes for your child and prevent them from ever experiencing harm, would you? Of course. If all of your efforts to control your child led to them living a safer, better life, would it be worth it? Of course! But what if some of your efforts to protect your child are backfiring, leading to:

- Your child becoming more distant and resistant to you

- Your feeling more stressed and anxious

- Your child missing out on important learning opportunities to enhance their sense of autonomy and self-reliance

Parenting doesn't have to be an endless tug-of-war with your child. You can drop the rope and opt out of the game. There are so many more interesting, fun-filled games you could be playing with your child. And you will both have the energy to engage in more meaningful, growth-inspiring interactions.

Parent Brain Rewiring Exercise: Ready to Drop the Rope?

Imagine for a moment that, on the count of 3, you could drastically decrease the amount of energy you are putting into trying to control your child's choices. Ready? 1, 2, 3! Would you be prepared to take us up on this offer?

Some questions to consider:

- Are you really ready to make this change?

- What fears or hesitations come up when you think about letting go of control?

- Are there any inner voices telling you otherwise? Do they sound protective, critical, or caring? Do they resemble your own role models, like a parent or a friend?

- Can you identify any rules you have about having to be in control as a parent?

- Do you see the benefit of decreasing your parenting control efforts, even if it feels difficult to take the plunge?

Let's see how Ali engaged in this exercise:

Nope. I do not feel ready to decrease the amount of parenting control I am striving for. It keeps my family safe. Why should I ditch it if I know that it helps protect us from the consequences of bad choices? I don't want my kids or my wife to feel like I let them down. I don't want them to feel what it's like to fail. What if he makes a terrible, life-altering decision—how could I live with myself knowing I didn't intervene and help him make a better choice? I can hear my father's voice telling me I am responsible for my family's well-being. A good parent would do everything they possibly can to protect their kids—that feels like a rule I have to live by. Benefits? I guess there would be less arguing. But that seems like a small price to pay for my peace of mind that things will work out well.

The Illusion of Control

When we ask our clients this same series of questions, they are usually quick to say yes, they would love to relinquish their need to control their children. They describe how exhausting it feels to be constantly assaulted by their overthinking brains and desperate efforts for control, all the while struggling to take pleasure in their parenting "wins." They are often game to eliminate this ineffective thinking style. But when we talk further about how this would actually play out in practical, daily life terms, they hesitate. Cue daunting fears: *If I accept the limits of my control, then I will be* [insert critical thought here]; *if I let go of control, then my child will be* [insert catastrophizing thought here].

It is a common belief that striving for control will help keep you and your loved ones safe and motivate you to take appropriate action. Many parents fear that allowing their child to choose rather than being told how to proceed, in various aspects of their life, will increase the odds of potentially disastrous outcomes. They fear that relinquishing parenting control will leave them feeling even more stressed, anxious, and worried for their child's current and future well-being. But the more you attempt to control, the more out of control you feel. And the tale of Ali, Zariah, and the dreaded snow pants is a perfect example.

Letting go of control in parent-child struggles can bring up concerns about being a "bad parent." Parents worry that if they don't exert control and protect their child against all negative consequences, they are failing. It takes effort to flip the script from seeing a parent's job as maintaining maximum control to seeing it as slowly shifting from control to support mode, once a child is old enough to learn how to manage select aspects of their life.

Relinquishing Control for Two

When you keep struggling with your child, trying to control their behavior, the struggle escalates and inevitably wears you both down. The quality of your relationship with your child is impacted with each tug-of-war for control. It's hard to be the parent you want to be when you feel exhausted and defeated. Your child may also resist seeking your support when they are struggling. Excessive parental control can leave children feeling judged. Feeling constantly criticized or overwhelmed by your frequent demands, they may want to hide from or avoid you.

When you instead accept the limits of your parenting control, you can drastically reduce this oppositional force between you and your child. When kids are accountable for their own choices, there is less resistance and more room for self-motivation. When your child knows you trust them to proceed, experiment, and adapt how they handle similar situations in the future, you enhance their sense of self and belief in their resiliency and ability to navigate life's challenges. Relinquishing control of certain parenting moments will bring you closer to your child. They will learn that you are there for them when they need you and that they can seek out your advice and guidance without feeling they must give up their autonomy.

Tolerating Discomfort and Uncertainty

Imagine you fall into a ditch with nothing but a shovel. The only thing you can focus on is getting yourself out as fast as possible. So you desperately try to shovel yourself out of the ditch. How is that going to go? Will you find yourself closer to freedom from the ditch, or dug in deeper? As unsatisfying as it may sound, at the very least, drop the shovel. Be still and accept your predicament. *Now* you can devote your mental energy to thinking through next steps, instead of desperately and ineffectively trying to dig your way out.

Accepting the limits of your parenting control means tolerating the uncertainty that comes with it. Not an easy feat, especially when it comes to the livelihood of your nearest and dearest. But you've already been doing this your whole life. You can handle uncertainty. Have you allowed yourself to realize this? When your parent brain is so set on staying in control, you may have trouble leaning into the lack of certainty at the core of human experience. But the flip side of uncertainty is wonder, whimsy, and delight. If you knew exactly what was going to happen next, how satisfying would your favorite book or movie have been?

Parent Brain Rewiring Exercise: Does Control Really Work for You?

Think of a frustrating moment in your life where you tried as hard as you could to change the outcome, but no matter what you did, the outcome was actually out of your control. Maybe a coworker was picked over you for a job promotion. Maybe your child decided to quit their soccer team, although you wanted them to keep playing because they had worked so hard at it for years and shown great potential. How much emotional energy did you put into fighting against what was already occurring?

Now think of a time when you accepted a frustrating situation where you couldn't change the outcome. Maybe it was a tense interaction about politics with your friend. Maybe your child chose to wear pajamas to school—but not on pajama day. By accepting the discomfort of a situation, you don't condone or agree with it; you allow it to be and acknowledge that fighting it would be ineffective and not worth your time or energy.

Which of these situations led to extra servings of stress and anxiety on top of inevitable feelings of frustration and disappointment?

Your Attempts for Control

The first step in shifting from control-based to support-based parenting is recognizing the different forms of control-based parenting you engage in and assessing which is backfiring, leading to more distance and less connection with your child.

Here are some common parenting control behaviors:

- Jumping in to rescue the child from age-appropriate challenges, or problem solving for them

- Peppering the child with questions, to make sure they are okay

- Telling the child to do things a specific way when there is a range of acceptable ways

- Repeatedly issuing the same command for them to perform the behavior when they ignore these prompts

- Offering advice or help when they have not asked for it

- Pointing out to the child all the negative consequences if they don't follow parental guidance

- Silently but clearly sending signals of judgment and disappointment when they choose to forge their own path with an age-appropriate decision

- Claiming "it is up to you" or asking them whether they would like to do something, but when they proceed differently, conveying disappointment and frustration in words or body language

Do you recognize any of these parenting control strategies? Are there any others you engage in that lead to emotionally exhausting, unproductive power struggles?

All of these behaviors are well intentioned and very common—so many of the wonderful, loving parent clients we work with find themselves engaging in these parenting control strategies. But there are three critical downsides:

- Your brain comes to identify your attempt to control your child's age-appropriate behaviors as necessary and to believe your child will face increasingly catastrophic consequences if they get it wrong.

- These approaches signal to your child that they are in danger and are not competent and strong enough to handle life without your protecting and guiding them. This eroding sense of self and over-reliance on others to manage all aspects of life is correlated with development of anxiety disorders in children and adolescents.

- Your investment of your precious time and mental energy in your relationship with your child not only generates no return but actually depletes your asset, chipping away at your connection with your child.

Parenting control behaviors may provide your brain with a bit of relief in the short term, as it responds to your amygdala signal *Something is wrong...the child will be cold...they may freeze to death in the next few minutes while building a snowman* by prompting an action: "Put on your snow pants." If you can get your child to engage in the behavior your brain has decided is necessary for their survival, your brain will calm down for a few moments, believing they are now safe. But the long-term message your brain gets is *If they did not listen to me and wear their snow pants, they would have experienced a catastrophic consequence. I must continue to make them follow my commands at all times or they will not survive.*

You are rewiring your brain to accept that you cannot (and need not) control all aspects of your child's life. When you allow your child to proceed without intervening, your brain learns that they are actually okay (albeit cold and wet). More moments like this allow your brain to experience how hardy and competent your child can be when left to fend for themself. Your brain can calm down, experience less stress and anxiety, and eventually rejoice in handing off more and more control to your child, freeing you to partner with them rather than micromanage them.

Making Acceptance Work for You

Acceptance does *not* mean desiring a negative outcome. For example, I can accept that I just stubbed my toe without being thrilled about the momentary throbbing pain. But it does mean I open up to the situation as it unfolds rather than fighting against what is. So instead of yelling at myself for being so clumsy and distracted that I never pay attention to my environment, and then experiencing even more discomfort on top of throbbing pain, I can just accept that I did stub my toe and now I need to move through the temporary pain. I can choose to not pile emotional discomfort on top of physical pain. This is psychological acceptance: opening up to the inevitable rather than fighting to change what cannot be changed.

The goal is to accept and lean into the situation, instead of struggling with it. Would it have been better if I hadn't stubbed my toe or if you could get your child to wear snow pants before going out to play in a blizzard? Absolutely yes on both fronts! Yet when you proactively choose acceptance, you free up your intellectual, emotional, and physical resources for aspects of life where you can create meaningful change.

> Ali was challenged to shift from seeing acceptance of limited parental
> control as laziness and avoidance to seeing it as an active approach of
> choosing how and when to invest his emotional energy. It took him several
> small experiments in allowing Lucas to make an expanded range of
> age-appropriate choices. Through these efforts, he came to experience
> firsthand how there is nothing passive about acceptance-based parenting. It

took strength and determination to let Lucas decide whether to eat the fruit cup before the chicken nuggets, even though Ali's brain was yelling The fruit is the dessert part of the meal. You must eat the chicken nuggets first! With each practice, Ali became more and more able to allow his son to experiment with making age-appropriate choices and tolerated the results, even when the outcomes differed from his brain's frantic directives.

Ali promised himself he'd apologize to Zariah for all his unfair and inaccurate parenting judgments. He now understood what was going on when his sister allowed Emmett to make certain choices for himself. When she opted to drop the rope and allow Emmett to choose how to proceed, such as during the snow pants incident, she was "relinquishing parental control." She wasn't too weak or lazy to make him put on his snow pants; she wanted him to experience the natural consequences of his choice. Ali had heard these words before, but they had just never clicked; it seemed more like an excuse for taking the easy way out. Experiencing for himself how much strength and fortitude it took to step back and let Lucas make certain choices for himself allowed Ali to better understand what it meant to be a good parent. A good parent knows when to maintain control but also is willing to selectively relinquish control so their child has the growth-enhancing experiences they need to become a responsible, self-reliant, confident adult.

When you selectively relinquish parenting control, you are acting with intention to drop the rope in that tug-of-war with your child. It takes strength and fortitude to accept and allow the situation your child is experiencing to unfold according to your child's preference—not yours. As it did for Ali, it may take a bit of playing and experimenting to get your brain to understand how selectively relinquishing parenting control is actually a show of strength, not weakness.

But shifting from control to acceptance-based parenting is not as easy as flipping a switch. Rewiring your parent brain to strive to control less and accept more of your child's behaviors may feel counterintuitive, scary, or even all-out wrong.

Parent Brain Rewiring Exercise: Misconceptions of Parenting Control

Do any of these beliefs about control keep you locked into engaging in power struggles with your child?

- If I try hard enough, I can make them see it my way.

- If I don't fight for control, I am showing my child they can make poor choices without consequences.

- I can't be a decent parent if I let my child do something without my guidance that could lead to negative consequences.

- My child will grow up to be reckless, inconsiderate, and [other undesirable attribute] if I just accept their choices.

Can you think of any additional beliefs about the value and necessity of control-based parenting that may be blocking your ability to test-drive acceptance-based parenting?

Parent Brain Rewiring Exercise: Why Is Acceptance Worth It to You?

Now that you know that struggling for seamless parenting control only leaves you feeling ineffective and trapped in a nonstop game of tug-of-war, let's explore all the meaningful moments that await you and your child if you rewire your brain to support and coach them rather than direct them through life.

- How would your relationship with your child look different?

- How would your relationship with your partner or family change?

- Which activities would you be doing more with your child?

- What aspect of parenting could you be more present for?

- What other important aspects of your life could you enjoy now?

Break Out of Power Struggles Through Acceptance

Even though from the outside it looked like Zariah glided through power struggles with Emmett, on the inside she still had to work on not giving in to the urge to rescue, correct, or control him as he encountered obstacles. For instance, she had recently allowed her son to invite a group of friends over to their house. The boys were excitable and loud, playing their favorite video games and grazing on tons of snacks. Zariah loved to see her son connecting with his friends (even if it was through screens sometimes). She was also relieved to find a break in the day to relax and listen to her favorite podcast while her younger daughter, Maya, was napping. However, her relaxing moments were soon interrupted by the boys screaming and cheering, as their opposing teams battled it out for top placement in whatever game they were playing. Zariah went downstairs every few minutes to remind the boys to keep the noise down. Each time the boys agreed, but within a few minutes the one overly excitable friend was yelling again. Zariah's frustration mounted. She was so irritated by this boy's lack of awareness and seemingly blatant disregard for the rest of her family. Every part of her wanted to storm downstairs, turn off the video game, and tell her son's friends to go home if they were going to be disrespectful and not listen.

Zariah had two choices: First, she could tell Emmett and the boys that they were out of chances to decrease their noise volume (in more kid-friendly lingo) and the playdate was now over. This would leave Emmett in a state of despair and anger for the rest of the day, which would do nothing to help Zariah fit a bit of "me time" into her day. Plus, Emmett would likely end up being heckled and taunted by his buddies, who seemed to be allowed to play video games at any volume, at any time, with minimal limits. She was not prepared to go that far in terms of her stance on video game usage but still wanted to him to fall somewhere within the social norms of their community.

Second, she could listen to her podcast with her headphones on and accept that if Maya woke up from her nap, it would not be the end of the world. Zariah had continued her daughter's midday nap routine for a bit too long, and this could be the nudge she needed to allow this inevitable developmental shift. Maya was already outgrowing this routine; it was becoming harder to persuade her to take a nap. Zariah had so enjoyed the quiet time that Maya's nap gave her, and she was in denial about the increasing struggles. It was time to allow acceptance-based parenting to work its magic: accepting both Emmett and his buddies' loud and rowdy playdates and the loss of that treasured midday relief she'd gotten when Maya napped.

Zariah chose to accept reality. Her son's friend was going to be loud, and reminders did not seem to help. Each time she went downstairs to try and control their noise level, to no avail, actually made her feel more powerless and ineffective. She focused on how much joy it brought her to see her son bonding and having fun with friends. By choosing acceptance, she recognized the limits and costs of striving for parental control. This also freed her to apply her energy to a more productive end—such as obtaining a new life hack from her podcast—rather than continuing to fight a losing battle against her children's quests for autonomy, which were each developmentally appropriate, albeit frustrating.

By practicing flexing your acceptance mental muscles, you too can learn to tolerate and move through the many uncontrollable moments of parenting and even find some wonder and delight in the chaos and uncertainty of it all. Strengthening your ability to relinquish parenting control is not just a philosophical shift; it takes ongoing, consistent practice of expanding your child's ability to make choices, while tolerating and not giving in to the incessant urge to correct, command, or rescue them.

Parent Brain Rewiring Exercise: Practicing Dropping the Rope

Imagine your child is whining and complaining about how they don't want to go to their piano lesson next week. You were just about to relax with a book before bed. You feel so frustrated. Your instinct is to set the record straight— "Lessons are paid for, and you will be taking them." Besides, you know that your child tends to whine about lessons in advance, but ends up going and returns feeling proud of their new skills. You have two choices:

1. Explain to your child, in a frustrated tone, how they have no choice but to go. If they continue to say they won't, remind them how you prepaid for the lessons; when we make a commitment, we need to follow through on the commitment. If one day they are to have a job and a roof over their head, they need to learn how to do things that are hard, even if they are tiring, stressful, or undesirable in any other way.

2. You acknowledge their frustration about having to go to their lesson, and you tell them that right before bed, a week before the lesson, is not the time to discuss this. You let them know you are willing to talk with them about their feelings about piano at a different time, but at this moment, it is time to unwind before bed.

Does the first option feel like the right choice? What do you anticipate happening next? Your child will probably keep trying to state their case to achieve their goal of not going. And you'll keep reminding them that you are in control and have decided for them. They then call you the "worst parent ever," and the debate keeps going until the two of you are exhausted. Now you and your child both feel the opposite of relaxed. It is going to be a long night...

Does the second option feel like a hard choice to make? Did you feel the discomfort in letting go of your attempt for control and the uncertainty of what may unfold? It might surprise you what could happen next. Your child will probably feel heard and validated. They don't need to fight for their case any more if you've expressed your understanding. And in that moment, you decide to acknowledge them but not concede to their request to be told they won't have to go to piano next week. Just because your child is seeking control in the moment does not mean you have to fight to retain it. You are the parent, and even if they are not acknowledging your authority, you still have it.

Parent Brain Rewiring Exercise: To Control or Not to Control

Part A: Over the course of a week, note in your Training Journal any parenting moments when you find yourself engaging in a power struggle with your child.

Whenever you feel the need to exert control over your child's actions, take the following steps:

1. Note how much distress you feel as you grasp for control, from 0 to 10.

2. Note any physical sensations of discomfort or catastrophic thoughts about either you as a parent or the situation.

3. Consider whether grasping for control of this particular moment brings you closer to your parenting values or not.

4. Assess how much danger your child would actually be in if you decided to drop the rope in this situation and allow them to choose how to proceed.

5. Look for any overall themes and patterns. What are the nuances and distinctions between the scenarios when your parent brain is willing to relinquish a bit more control to your child and the ones when your brain struggles to loosen the reins and allow for child-guided decision making?

What did you notice about your willingness to assign situations in which to drop the rope? Which fears showed up for you? Did you notice your parent brain trying to justify why you shouldn't let go of control over select areas? Did you notice the difference between reason-based choosing to maintain maximum parental control over a sphere of your child's life and those that were more fear-based reactions? What did it feel like in your body when your emotionally reactive, amygdala-activated mind anxiously pointed out something you *must continue to do or else something catastrophic will happen* compared with times when your reason-based, PFC-activated mind, guided by your parenting values, declared that your child is not yet ready to make a decision that could have irreversible long-term consequences.

Part B: This exercise will help you further clarify that certain aspects of your child's life are nonnegotiables for you now, and that, based on your parenting values and beliefs, you will continue as decision maker until they reach future developmental milestones. This exercise will also help you identify healthy challenge zones for you to practice relinquishing control and for your child to practice greater personal responsibility and learn from the consequences of their decisions.

In your Training Journal, draw three circles: the three buckets of control.

1. In bucket #1, list problems you encounter with your child that (1) annoy you and you wish your child didn't do, and (2) are beyond your control.

    •   Although frustrating, these issues are not worth your efforts or the conflicts with your child that are inevitable as you fight for control. You can tolerate the discomfort that comes with these issues.

    •   Examples: choosing an unhealthy snack, cracking knuckles, forgetting to make their bed, not finishing the activity they started, cutting piano practice short

2. In bucket #2, list problems you encounter with your child that (1) you worry may lead to problematic behaviors in the future and (2) do not *flexibly* align with your family's values system. (Your child can choose values different from the family's values [e.g., on religion], so it's important to be flexible. However, common human core values [like kindness] are ones that you can work to guide your child toward.)

    •   You can step in and redirect your child to more adaptive behaviors; however, you allow your child to learn through natural consequences and build intrinsic motivation to change (if they eventually choose to do so). You can tolerate the uncertainty.

    •   Examples: not going to bed on time, not studying for a test, choosing unfavorable friends, making rude comments to a peer

3. In bucket #3, list any problems that are a safety concern.

- These are nonnegotiable; you can step in and take control. Here, your energy could be used effectively.

- Examples: running away, aggressive behaviors, failing in school

Sometimes it's helpful to recognize how you would react if the roles were reversed. Think back to a time when someone was trying to control your choices. Maybe when you were younger you had a parent adamant that you choose a business major in college, when you wanted to focus your studies on art history. How did that pressure feel? How did that affect your motivation and excitement about college? Maybe it made you even more determined to make your own choice, or maybe it filled you with guilt and confusion. Let's say you chose your major anyway—were you equipped to handle any issues that came up later? Of course you were—there were lessons learned, and you figured it out. Now, from your perspective as a parent yourself, you can see that your parents probably just wanted to ensure your success and security in life. So even though you may have made your own choice—despite your parents' well-intentioned urge to control the steps you would take on your life path—did their value in life entail being your ultimate teacher of how to live effectively? Was there a better way for you to learn this life lesson other than living it out firsthand?

Your Child's Brain on Enhanced Autonomy

Teaching your parent brain to have more trust in your child's capabilities does not guarantee they will make the right choices all the time (as that is impossible for any of us). This also doesn't mean that they will be protected from all negative consequences. But what it does allow for is no less remarkable. By selectively relinquishing parenting control and allowing your child to expand their autonomy in a developmentally appropriate manner, you signal to them that you believe in them and see them as a competent, resilient person. Each time they choose how to proceed (rather than soldier on, following your orders), they enhance their effective decision-making mental circuitry. With each right choice they learn how to make similar choices, and with each wrong choice they learn to avoid a negative outcome at the next fork in the path. And your child's boosted confidence and sense of self are powerful assets for establishing and maintaining a safe, productive life. So even if they end up occasionally wet and cold, or have to stay in during recess because they did not finish their homework, learning they can pick themselves up and move past these and similar obstacles will set them up for a lifetime of effective problem solving and healthy coping. And as they make additional decisions as appropriate for their age, not only does your child benefit, but also your parent brain will experience less stress and anxiety and more shared moments of joy, wonder, and delight.

Parent Brain Rewiring Exercise: Create Your Personalized Relinquishing Parenting Control Plan

Time to put it all together. We will guide you through creating a customized parenting plan that makes it easier for you and your child to navigate around power struggles. Now you can consciously decide when you will relinquish decision-making authority to them and when you will hold on to control until they have had more time to grow and mature. In your Training Journal, reflect on the following:

- Your child's temperament, unique characteristics, and strengths

- Your own temperament and parenting strengths

- Your family and cultural values

- Societal events that may contribute to your parenting approach

- Any coparenting challenges and opportunities for growth

- Any personal challenges that might interfere with your parenting practices

Based on your answers, commit to working your "relinquishing parental control" mental muscles once a day. You need not make a 180-degree shift from maintaining maximum parental control to acceptance-based parenting to see rapid gains. You can take small (but significant) steps toward embracing acceptance, such as letting your child make a choice about their after-school snack or which shoes to wear to school. Remember, the goal is not to have you drop them off the side of a cliff with no parachute. Think of this process as building a secure and reliable parachute together.

How These Acceptance Exercises Rewire Your Parent Brain to Reduce Stress and Anxiety

When you channel excessive mental and emotional energy into trying to control the uncontrollable, you end up stressed out, exhausted, and frustrated. And all of this hard work will only move you further away from becoming the effective and compassionate parent you hope to be. Instead, you can identify developmentally appropriate opportunities for your child to expand their autonomy and practice making effective decisions. These give your child invaluable life lessons in the (small but meaningful) consequences of effective as well as ineffective decision making. They also help your parent brain clarify and articulate the aspects of your child's life that are currently nonnegotiable. Once your child knows you mean what you say and you say what you mean, they will naturally engage in fewer power struggles. They can tell when you mean business and you are not going to budge—and when there is wiggle room and you will let them have their way if they bug you enough. You might as well decide from the start where you stand on relinquishing control over different spheres of life; then there will be much less stress and anxiety for all parties. And with less time spent engaging in power struggles with your child, you will have more energy to devote to living your best life and teaching your child how to do the same.

CHAPTER 8

Living Out Your Values

This story of two mothers may be familiar and helpful if your kids participate in school athletics—or any other all-consuming extracurricular pursuit.

Mona and Jen each had a son; both sons were juniors in high school. The boys were passionate and skilled hockey players on the school's varsity team. The mothers were proud of their sons' determination and commitment to the sport. Mona and Jen were also highly invested in the sport—they drove their sons to every practice and game and often traveled for hockey tournaments. They both worked hard to nurture their sons' passion for playing the game.

Jen struggled with finding time for herself. Between packing snacks, driving to games, and keeping up with her own professional life, she often felt drained after a long week. She couldn't understand how other parents seemed to have it all together. Putting 100 percent effort into everything wasn't sustainable. She could sense her spouse starting to feel neglected. She could tell that her coworkers were feeling annoyed with multiple missed deadlines. But Jen knew how much her son, Noah, loved hockey, and she loved helping him prioritize his practice. She shared his excitement with every goal he scored and his team camaraderie. She wanted to be there every step of the way. When he felt accomplished, so did she. When he missed the game-saving goal and felt defeated, she felt his pain. She brought snacks for parents, organized hockey trips, and cared for the team like they were family. Jen poured her heart and soul into making anything possible for her son's athletics because it was so important to him. And if it was important to him, it was important to her.

Mona, too, would feel emotionally and physically spent after a week of work, managing kids' school schedules, and hockey practice drop-offs and pick-ups. One Friday, she realized that she had been so busy earlier in the week that she hadn't made any time for herself. She felt some relief in figuring out why the heck she felt so drained. Mona had learned the hard way that if she didn't take care of herself and get to what mattered to her at some point in the week, everything else in her life would feel more chaotic and unmanageable. While Mona strived to be a wonderful mother, she knew she needed to balance this important role with other valued parts of her life. She was also an adventure seeker who loved musicals, baking, and the outdoors. Mona knew that all these parts of herself were integral to feeling energized and fulfilled.

So what to do? Neither mom was ready to devote less time to their sons' athletics. In fact, that idea deflated them even more—they loved to join in on all aspects of their sons' hockey endeavors. However, while Jen was narrowly locked into her one value, centered on her child, Mona recognized that she needed to tend to other important parts of herself.

Jen's Parent Brain Default State: Child-Centered Living

For Jen, the problem wasn't that she prioritized Noah's athletics—it was that she overly prioritized his athletics. After a week of managing his hockey affairs (not to mention taking care of her family and work), she felt exhausted and perhaps a wee bit resentful. While she knew being involved in Noah's hockey career was important to her, the exhaustion gradually gained more footing than her excitement. Jen judged herself for not being as committed as the other hockey moms. She couldn't understand how they could make time for everything else and still be so involved with their children. She felt ashamed that she couldn't keep up with what others made it look so easy to juggle. The idea of making time for herself, a notion often pushed onto her by others, created instant guilt. For Jen, just the thought of prioritizing her own needs was tied to feeling like a bad mom. She didn't want to contribute in any way to Noah's feeling unsupported. What if he resented her for her selfishness and their relationship suffered? Worried *about these potential catastrophic scenarios, she continued to neglect herself and all of her personal goals and priorities.*

Mona's Parent Brain Default State: Valued Living

For Mona, having well-balanced priorities helped her feel more energized and present for the important aspects of her life. By participating in activities she loved that fell outside of the parenting sphere, she maintained a sense of self and purpose. Knowing she had so little time, Mona set out to infuse small daily doses of her personal values throughout her week. For instance, during the twenty-minute drive to hockey practice, she blared her favorite songs from Hamilton—even though her son, Ethan, rolled his eyes and put on his headphones. If Mona arrived to pick him up early from practice, she might get out of the car and sit on a bench to enjoy the fresh air. Sure, the hockey practice parking lot wasn't exactly a national park, but on a busy weekday, time spent in the fresh air satisfied her love of the outdoors just enough. In these moments, Mona felt like she had just filled up her imaginary gas tank, helping herself to be revitalized and ready to take on what life had in store for her.

Both moms were committed to being engaged and supportive in their children's passions. While Jen kept putting more and more into Noah and his ever-expanding hockey needs, it still never felt like enough. She couldn't seem to shake the feeling that she should be a better mom. Yet the harder she tried to make herself available, the more exhausted she got and the worse she seemed to be doing as a mother.

In contrast, Mona accepted her limitations. Yes, she was committed to her son's hockey life, but she knew she had to make room for herself if she was going to stay excited and present as a mother. She needed to pace herself and her energy reserve to maintain her sense of balance and life satisfaction.

You have likely encountered similar challenges when attempting to manage and engage in both your child's life and your own. As you read about Jen and Mona, perhaps your own parent brain tried to offer explanations or excuses for why you are not making room for your own wants or needs.

This chapter will help you learn to:

- Identify and reconnect with what enhances your sense of vitality

- Recognize your current patterns that interfere with making room for your own needs

- Create a realistic, balanced lifestyle that incorporates the things that are important to both you and your child

- Intentionally commit to engaging in behaviors and activities in line with your personal values

The Thrills and Spills of Child-Centered Living

When living a child-centered life, the thrills can feel so intensely wonderful. You can watch the joy your child feels at learning a new skill or ordering their favorite food. When your child is thriving, you are overcome with joy and delight. But the flip side is also true. Their spills become *your* (heart-wrenching) spills. Your child's pain becomes your pain. When child-centered living is what you know and do best, you *really* feel all of it. It is not uncommon for a parent to become so intertwined with their child's experience that they begin to lack a sense of individuation.

Individuation refers to the process by which you develop your own sense of self separate from the identities of others. It may feel like being a good parent requires fully attending to your child's desires over your own. But there is a cost, certainly to you but also to your child, when you neglect your own needs and put all of your energy and emotional resources into their lived experience. Research has found that overly involved parenting, which occurs when parents overidentify with a child's feelings and needs, can lead to increased childhood depression and anxiety (Yap et al., 2014). It is a huge weight for a child to carry, to feel they are responsible for your joy and life satisfaction. They need to know that you are okay on your own and it is therefore safe for them to explore and grow, even as they move further from you with each day they gain competence and maturity. They also need the freedom to make mistakes and get things wrong and to not feel that each struggle they experience will cause you undue harm.

We aren't suggesting that you always put your needs ahead of your child's needs. We are encouraging you to play around with a different approach to living a valued life. One that feels fulfilling and true to you, as a unique individual as well as a parent. With this in mind, we want you to move toward your needs, even when your anxious parent brain may try to convince you that doing so is selfish or wrong.

Values-Centered Parenting

Values are the fundamental beliefs that guide your actions and outlook on life—the things that matter the most to you and give your life meaning. Values allow you to move freely through life feeling rejuvenated and energized enough to tackle the next challenge that awaits you. The goal of values-centered parenting is to balance your needs and the needs of your child(ren). It's knowing when it is time to pause and refill your own gas tank so that you can successfully power through difficult moments. Valued living is a sustainable lifestyle that works to help you and your child feel fulfilled in the long run.

What does it mean to feel fulfilled, anyway? You can think of fulfillment as living a deeply meaningful life full of purpose and satisfaction. You can decide what that means for you. Note that this definition does not mention happiness. The goal is to not to be happy—that is completely unrealistic and unattainable, because every human emotion ebbs and flows. Society has hardwired our brains to continually strive for happiness, a common misconception that sets most people up for failure. But you can absolutely revel in those cherished moments of happiness as you fully reap the benefits of your best life.

Valued Living for Two

One important way to enhance individuation is to further define your own identity. Explore what matters to you most, and lean into what makes you uniquely you. The time you spend caring for yourself and your own values will have benefits far beyond the positive effects you feel from living your values. Your children can directly benefit from the ways you live a values-centered life.

By tending to your own wants and needs, you are actually modeling important life skills and healthy habits for your children.

When your children observe the way you embrace who you are and prioritize the things that matter most to you, they see someone who is authentically themself and confident in who they are. Even if your children can't directly relate to your passion for nature, cooking shows, or Broadway musicals, they see the way you prioritize your interests and embrace your unique self. They see the importance of being oneself and honoring one's values and interests. By giving yourself permission to indulge in the things that energize you and bring you joy, you give your children permission to do the same.

Parent Brain Rewiring Exercise: All About *You*

 The following questions are intended to prompt your self-reflection. In your Training Journal, take a moment to jot down your thoughts. Don't think too long about any question; write what first comes to mind. Bonus challenge: Complete a "speed round" and answer in one minute.

1. Who am I?

2. What do I value?

3. What makes life worth living for me?

4. When did I last feel fulfilled?

   - What was I doing?

   - How did I feel?

Did anything surprise you about your answers? When was the last time you thought about these things? Did your mind go completely blank and come up with nothing? Or maybe your child's needs kept popping up? Whatever your experience, we are only at the starting point.

Your parent brain will benefit from these reminders when life gets hectic. Write down a keyword or phrase that will remind you of your value(s) on a sticky note and place it somewhere you will see it when it matters most.

Feeling Lost?

We often hear from our wonderful parent clients that there is a sense of loss in the transition to parenthood. The things that used to matter to them no longer take precedence. Parents' needs get set on the back burner. It makes complete sense—those early stages of infancy and childhood demand this! Your life feels like it truly becomes centered around your child. And yet, while priorities may be reshuffled, you don't have to lose yourself in the shuffle. We gently remind our parent clients (and our parent readers) that "*You* are a priority, too."

As you read this chapter, your anxious parent brain might offer up thoughts similar to:

- *Why didn't anyone tell me this earlier?*

- *Do I even have any of my own values?*

- *I can't remember what used to be important to me.*

- *I feel this uncomfortable sense of guilt—it's wrong to prioritize myself.*

It can be tough to access your values, especially when your brain may have pushed them away in favor of only focusing on your child's experiences. It may have been a while since you thought through what matters most to you. This was certainly the case for Jen. She was so wrapped up with Noah's interests and goals that she did not feel connected to her own. When you start to connect more with the activities that are important in your life, you begin to anchor yourself to your authentic identity—one that includes being a parent, but also highlights all other aspects of your unique being.

Of course, most everyone goes through moments in life where they may not feel particularly purposeful or fulfilled. This is to be expected. What's important is that you are in touch with your values and can envision the life you want to be living. Commit to doing what makes you, you.

The exercises in this chapter will help you move closer to your very best values-centered life. Knowing what matters to you is the first step. You have the strength to balance the stuff that matters to you *and* the stuff that matters to your child. With this balance, you will reenergize and revitalize not only yourself but also your relationship with your child.

Your Parent Brain on Valued Living

With child-centered living, your emotions, fulfillment, and purpose depend on your child. Everything feels much more intense as your mirror neurons ramp up your reactions and, in turn, activate your amygdala. This is especially true if your brain is on high alert for *Am I making my child happy at all times?* Your anxiety will likely skyrocket if your goal is to configure an emotional experience not entirely in your control.

All of this makes it much harder to parent the way you want to. Your amygdala's sole purpose is to rescue your child (and yourself) from this awful, seemingly dangerous experience. However, your child may actually need something else. It's tough to equip your child with helpful problem-solving skills when your own amygdala is hijacked by your child's emotions. And when your parent brain is hyperfocused on your child's values (what matters most to them), it can be hard to provide a helpful perspective that could empower them to work through their challenges. Instead of accessing your PFC to think of and execute ways to support your child, you are both feeling stuck in the emotional discomfort. And feeling stuck precludes those fulfilling parenting moments you long for.

When you engage in authentic valued living, your amygdala is less activated because you have a greater sense of control in your own life. Research shows that living according to your values, and in turn not avoiding the pain that may surface, can actually decrease anxiety (Michelson et al., 2011). With your values guiding you toward meaningful action, your amygdala is no longer preparing for the potential dire consequences that loom when your focus is on avoiding your child's or your own discomfort.

So What *Actually* Matters to You?

Now that you know the benefits of valued living, does it make it any easier to jump right in? Maybe not just yet. First comes reflecting on your core values to create a clear picture of what is most important to you.

Values, and your commitment to living them, will ebb and flow in importance throughout your life. Jen could remember when she used to love going on hikes. She would leave work early and explore new trails. Her values—adventure and nature—helped her prioritize these experiences. Your values can provide a sense of purpose. They help you create your own narrative about who you are and what you want out of life. Sigh of relief! You aren't just an on-call coordinator of your child's valued activities. You get to align with your own, too.

Parent Brain Rewiring Exercise: Choose Your Own *Valued* Adventure

You are going on a *valued* adventure. You decide where to go, what to do, and who will be there. All the important stuff. Really envision your best day ever, one that gives you the warm fuzzy feelings of joy, satisfaction, and fulfillment. Bring your vision to life—what do you hear, feel, see, smell, taste? You might even close your eyes and take another sigh of relief…lean into this feeling, whatever comes up.

- **Choice 1:** Do you stay in this vision of your best life?

  You stay there. Enjoy yourself, you deserve it.

- **Choice 2:** Do you find it difficult to stay in this vision of your best life and/or quickly stop thinking about it?

  You stop there. It's tough to stay right now. You deserve to come back here, but you choose to first practice using your favorite tools from chapters 2 and 3.

Parent Brain Rewiring Exercise: Pick a Value, Any Value (well, the important ones)

Open your web browser and search for "values list." Simple enough, right? Settle on a website or image of your choice. Start picking your values:

1. Read through the list.

2. Write down at least fifteen to twenty of the values most important to you in your Training Journal. (Try to really home in on those that are

authentic to you, not those of your child, friends, family, or anyone else.)

3. Circle your top ten values—the ones that *really* matter the most (even though they all matter).

4. Highlight your top five values (from your circled items).

5. On a separate page, write, draw, or even papier-mâché your top five values for display.

6. Place your top five values "masterpiece" in a place where you will encounter it often.

Take a moment to reflect on the parts of these exercises that came easily to you and the more difficult moments, if any. In clarifying your values, your brain got to both intuitively and analytically explore the hidden pleasures and possible pain points of your best life. As you can probably tell, to take in all of the good, you learn to embrace the discomfort.

Caution: Watch Out for Hidden "Should" Values

Pause and reflect on your past week. Were there ups and downs, highs and lows? Or did all your plans run smoothly, assisted by a constant pleasant mood and stress-free parenting? The obvious answer to this is the former (such is life)—so why do we keep expecting the latter? Many parents hold themselves to unrealistic expectations, or 'shoulds,' that are often not a one-size-fits-all.

When Jen's son came home from school before his evening study group, she would often think *We should be doing something productive, like talking about his day or planning the week ahead*. She could feel the anxiety build as her resistance kicked in. Did she really have to be productive at that moment? Knowing she had limited emotional bandwidth from a busy week, the thought of "pulling teeth" from Noah (who would probably be fine without it) exhausted her even more. The conflict in her mind led her to shut down, and before she knew it, he had to leave for his group. Now she hadn't gotten to enjoy her limited time with her son and was stuck feeling anxious and regretful.

These should values are imposed on us by our own families, other families, societal messages—they are everywhere. Our minds are filled with constant shoulds: *I should have organized my time better this week* or *They should have listened to me, then we wouldn't be in this mess!* How productive are those thoughts, besides serving you a heaping dose of guilt or frustration? Do they help you move closer to your values in an authentic manner—or push you further from them?

Parent Brain Rewiring Exercise: Fill-in-the-Blank Parenting

Part A: Look through this list of attributes, then respond to the prompts that follow by selecting your top five choices, or add your own.

Accepting	Involved
Attentive	Loving
Authentic	Kind
Brave	Nurturing
Compassionate	Opinionated
Cool	Protective
Fair	Reliable
Fun	Sane
Generous	Smart
Giving	Strict
Hardworking	Strong
Honest	Supportive
Inspiring	Thoughtful

1. What type of parent do you *want* to be?

    - "I *want* to be a _____ parent." (Repeat four times, with different attributes.)

    - Notice how you feel: a bit of excitement, maybe motivation to do things that align with your wants?

2. What type of parent do you think you *should* be?

    - "I *should* be a _____ parent." (Repeat four times, with different attributes.)

    - Notice how you feel: some frustration, maybe guilt, or panic that you need to immediately change your parenting ways? (You don't!)

Part B: Did any of your *should* choices match up with your *want* choices?

- If yes, great! Keep those traits top of mind and see if you can incorporate them into your parenting.

- If not, great! Acknowledge the *should* values and see if you can tell where they come from (inner critic voice, your parent, a friend?). Now refocus your efforts on your *want* values and incorporate them into your parenting.

Remember that parenting shoulds are not helpful or productive when they don't align with your values. If something is not important to you or your child, but you feel a *should* guilting you into an undesired behavior, that's your cue to call the should police on your anxious parent brain. You can peacefully remind it that it is not helpful at the moment, but you appreciate its concerns.

The Stuff That Matters to Your Child

Your child is important to you. You have a lot of love to give. We know that, because you have this book in your hands and you continue to learn more ways to manage this valued relationship with your child. Your taking a sincere interest in your child's values reaps benefits for their growth and identity development. Research demonstrates many benefits for children whose parents are involved in their academic learning, including positive educational outcomes and positive social interactions with peers and other trusted adults (e.g., Fan & Chen, 2001; El Nokali et al., 2010). A healthy level of parental involvement also fosters a healthy attachment and a close relationship with you. Overinvolvement, however, is associated with poor outcomes for children. For instance, too much parental involvement can deter children from building essential self-regulation skills and independence (Obradović et al., 2021). Not to mention it takes a significant toll on parents' own mental health.

"I just want my child to be happy" is a common parental sentiment. Of course you do! Both Mona and Jen could attest to this. However, we challenge you to think about what you want your child's life to be about. Shift away from the impermanent emotion of happiness and toward values you'd like your child to make room for in their lives. We suggest, "I wish for my child to have a full and meaningful life." When you fully engage in your own valued living, not only do you teach your child the importance of this engagement, but you also get to fulfill this desire for your own life.

Parent Brain Rewiring Exercise: Your Child's Important Stuff

In your Training Journal, create a list of five things that you believe are important to your child. You can even ask your child. Their responses could include:

Valued activities (playing sports, games with family, going to school)

Valued traits (sense of humor, kindness, honesty)

Next, rate how important each valued activity and trait is to *you* on a scale of 0 to 10. Remember, we are asking about *your* values here, not how much you value your child's interest in the activity.

Now rate how much of your energy, time, or effort you devote to ensure your child experiences each of these values, from 0 to 100 percent.

- Notice the similarity or difference between your importance rating and your percentage rating.

- Which of your child's values did you align with?

- Which of your child's values were not so important to you?

It is a true strength to care intensely about your child's life experiences and be completely invested in them. But when your world starts to revolve *only* around their life (while yours is tossed to the side), we urge caution. Loving your child does not have to mean their "leading" your life, or that your needs don't matter. After all, you are not a parent robot. You need to feel joy, meaningful connection, and a sense of purpose for yourself in a variety of ways.

Commit to Doing What Matters to You

We don't want you to just know what is important to you; we want you to take action and fully engage in valued living. Infuse what's important to you into your daily routine, your weekends, your special moments and celebrations. Don't be daunted; this doesn't have to take up all your time. Find some activities that take a few minutes and others that require a few hours. With a bit of creativity and thought, you'll find a range of balanced activities that work with your schedule and are a good fit for you and your family.

Do what matters, with intention. Mona did this when she decided to blast *The Greatest Showman* soundtrack on her drive home from work, even though she felt the pull of anxiety telling her she needed to plan her to-dos for the next day. Valued living requires intentional commitment to an action plan that works for you. You are allowed to prioritize your values. When you are on your valued path, cultivating intention will come naturally. However, if you are noticing any unwelcome shoulds, this may be a sign that you are on the wrong valued path for *you*.

When your life is full of things that matter to you, your parent brain will be better equipped to tolerate any anxiety or discomfort. Be flexible with yourself and your time. It is normal and perfectly okay if you don't follow your plan judiciously. Use self-compassion to acknowledge when it is time to rein in your efforts, which may include giving yourself a break. Bonus points if that matches up to another one of your values, in which case—there you go, living your valued life.

Parent Brain Rewiring Exercise: Your Personal Values Action Plan

In your Training Journal, recall your top five values. For each value, think about things you can do to incorporate them into your life:

- Pick two activities that can be completed in thirty minutes or less.

- Pick two activities that require over thirty minutes to fully experience.

- Pick one activity that you can enjoy with your child.

- List a few rewards you can give yourself after following through with your plan.

Take a look at an example from Mona's Personal Values Action Plan:

Value: Humor

Short Action:

1. Listen to a comedy podcast.

2. Share a funny story with a friend over text.

Long Action:

1. Enjoy a night out at a comedy show.

2. Watch a funny movie.

With my son: Ask him to tell me a joke or riddle.

Rewards: Get a coffee, go for an extra-long walk, browse online stores.

During the coming week, try to engage in at least one valued activity every day. Enlist a friend to join you, or schedule specific times in your calendar to help keep yourself committed. Give yourself kudos for still having intentionally moved toward a valued life, even though your anxious parent brain may have been along for the ride.

So Many Values, So Little Time: A Balancing Act

You are living a life in which your values and your child's values coexist. Both desires are true and valid for each of you. Finding the happy medium as a parent requires flexibility and balance. We know it's not easy. And it depends on your child's life stage; when they are still majorly reliant on you it is probably more difficult to actively live your values.

As long as you are willing to try, you can live a life that honors both your and your child's values. Flexibility is key. Of course, life happens, and there will always be ups and downs. At times your schedule will be overtaken by your child's needs and commitments. The important thing is that your priorities don't get completely lost in the mix. Call on support from loved ones to help you stay balanced in your own needs and values. Be flexible in tending to your child's life thrills and spills, while making sure you can always find your way back to your own valued living path.

Parent Brain Rewiring Exercise: Your Shared Values Action Plan

In your Training Journal, create a list of five or more values that are important to both you and your child—your shared values. You can sit down together and look through a values list as you did earlier in the chapter. Now identify one or two actions or activities that align with each shared value. Schedule a time in the next week to complete at least one of these together.

Here is an example from Jen's Shared Values Action Plan she created with her son:

Value: Creativity

Short Action:

1. Leave a quick doodle on the fridge sticky notes; take turns adding.

2. Sit outside together and take turns asking questions.

Long Action:

1. Cook dinner together and try a new recipe.

2. Do an art project together.

Scheduled for: Cook dinner together tomorrow night

After the week, reflect on what it felt like to create this balance in valued living with your child. Any surprises, challenges, unexpected ease? Anxious parent brain noise? Notice if any roadblocks get in the way, and add in supports to keep you accountable. Rinse and repeat!

Welcome Your Anxious Parent Brain When It Shows Up

You are now well equipped to make some meaningful changes in your life. So let's not be surprised when your anxious parent brain tries to interfere. After all, it's just trying to protect you. Acknowledge the uncomfortable feelings and recognize the false alarm your amygdala is trying to sound. As long as you remain willing and focused on the person you want to be and the life you want to live, your values will help guide you through the discomfort. Your newly rewired brain neuroconnections will make your effort easier.

Remember, your anxiety is really the flip side of your core values as a parent, fueled by your immense love for your child. So of course it will show up when you stray away from child-centered living. Jen's anxious parent brain would usually overwhelm her with dramatic (and unhelpful) cautionary tales, like *If your son, the one you love most, gets mad at you, how will you live with yourself!?* or *What if you're out gallivanting, doing your values, and something bad happens to your kid!?* Super uncomfortable. But recall that this kind of child-centered living did not work for Jen, and probably not for you either. Instead, use your tools to tolerate these anxious thoughts while also feeling fulfilled doing the things you love.

How These Values Clarification Exercises Rewire Your Parent Brain to Reduce Stress and Anxiety

Rewiring your parent brain to experience less stress and anxiety is difficult work. Child-centered living trains your amygdala to be on high alert and feel out of control, whereas valued living brings a greater sense of control, decreased amygdala activity, and lower anxiety overall. There may be times when your brain anxiously reminds you of the importance of attending to your child's values in spite of your own values. If this comes up for you, remember:

- Balance is key—there is room for both your values.

- Living a fulfilled and meaningful life benefits everyone.

- Living out your values takes intentional commitment.

- Making room for your values opens you up to feeling energized and satisfied instead of exhausted and emotionally depleted.

CHAPTER 9

Perfectly Imperfect Parenting

We parents are subject to so much societal pressure and imagery demanding perfection. Let's see how Talia and Imani handled this challenge.

Talia and Imani were two moms who worked as teachers at the same elementary school. Over the past few months, they had become close friends and often swapped stories about parenting and teaching. They'd share their weekly "fails," like losing their lesson plans in the shuffle, or almost driving away from the house to drop off their kids at school with no kids in the car. They bonded over the thrills and spills of work/life balance as they attempted to do it all as both teachers and parents.

Outside of work, Talia and Imani sent each other parenting tips and relatable memes through social media. Imani would poke fun at "social media moms" boasting about their flawless and perfect lives. Talia would be quick to laugh, but secretly felt overwhelmed and defeated by the idea of other moms having it all together. Still, both Talia and Imani felt connected through the shared chaos of parenting two young children while also working full time.

One Friday during their lunch break, Talia broke down in tears. She felt like she had failed at everything that week: she lost her keys and was late to work, forgot to pack her daughter's lunch, missed the deadline to sign her son up for swimming lessons, and ended up ordering takeout for dinner almost every night. Talia was completely overwhelmed—she felt like she was dropping balls left and right in her efforts to juggle so many competing demands. She felt the pressure to keep up with family responsibilities, and the thought that she was letting her family down was consuming her mind and making it difficult for her to concentrate at work.

In an effort to ease Talia's guilt, Imani jokingly pointed out that Talia was helping to teach her kids how to be "perfectly imperfect." Imani explained how that particular life skill would get them much further than any missed home-cooked meal or swimming lesson. Talia laughed, but the guilt remained. She knew she lived a blessed life with a loving partner and a stable income, and she was convinced that it shouldn't be so difficult for her to hold it together and keep her family's life running smoothly.

Imani felt her friend's pain. It's not easy or even feasible to keep every aspect of life perfectly in place. She knew this firsthand—sometimes things not going according to plan felt like the rule rather than the exception. Imani told Talia that she too had weeks when it seemed like one mistake after another, day after day. Just last month, Imani had felt like an epic failure of a mother when her daughter had to miss out on a class baking activity because she'd forgotten to buy the ingredients. That same day, her son's teacher called to discuss his tardiness, which she knew was because of Imani's waking up late. As Imani shared her parenting troubles, Talia felt confused—she remembered hearing about this from Imani before, but she had shared it all so casually. At the time, Talia thought Imani seemed to be okay with the chaos and mishaps in her family life.

Imani knew that this was far from the truth. She didn't feel good about her parenting mishaps, but she was willing to feel the resulting disappointment and frustration. She knew those feelings were a part of the parenting experience. Still, it wasn't easy. Imani worked hard to give herself permission to make mistakes. Instead of labeling her experiences as failures, she took them as an opportunity to change and continue learning. When feelings of guilt and failure began to surface, she knew it was time to slow down and ground herself in her values. By reminding herself what she wants her life to be about, she found it easier to let the little things go. Her energy (a precious and limited parenting resource) was better spent on moments with her family and students. Imani decided she could be more effective overall by sometimes deciding to do less and accept good enough instead of trying to be perfect.

Talia's Parent Brain Default State: Chasing Perfection

For Talia, aspiring for perfection at work and home led her to feel even more imperfect. Imani was so shockingly carefree when admitting to her parenting mistakes! The thought of failing as a parent haunted Talia; she had always planned to do and be the very best she could for her kids. Ever since her first pregnancy, Talia had filled her shelves with parenting books, and she filled her social media outlets with parenting resources, from mommy blogs to alleged parenting experts. Her well-intentioned effort soon became a shame spiral. Whenever Talia took a short pause from the busyness of life, she scrolled through social media and was quickly inundated with seemingly perfect families and parenting propaganda. Those other parents could do it all for their kids, so why couldn't she? As she scrolled, Talia agonized over the awful impact she might have on her children's lives. She got so caught up in her worries that she often zoned out while Imani shared her own struggles as a mother. And even though she knew Imani made parenting mistakes too, they didn't seem as regrettable, since Imani so easily laughed it off and moved on to another topic. Talia couldn't understand why she felt like such a terrible mother when she was trying so hard to avoid messing up. It was exhausting.

Imani's Parent Brain Default State: Perfectly Imperfect

For Imani, being flexible with her own expectations preserved the emotional bandwidth to handle whatever life threw her way. Did disappointments feel any better? No, but she didn't have to live in that feeling for very long. Through her hard work, her parent brain has learned how to accept, acknowledge, and learn from her mistakes, to tolerate and move through to-be-expected parenting mishaps. Imani also wanted to be the best possible mother to her children and teacher to her students, but she knew that best had to have a more realistic and sustainable meaning than perfect. Imani worked hard to be gentle and flexible in her own parenting expectations. It wasn't easy to balance all the wishes she had for her children's future with realistic expectations—it actually felt terrifying. Even so, Imani continued to tolerate her natural parenting imperfections. The initial discomfort was so worth the time she could actually be present in all areas of her life, especially with her children. Imani found it was easier to sit with the discomfort of making mistakes when she could laugh about it with a trusted friend.

Talia and Imani both wanted to be the best possible parent for their children. While Talia felt defeated by this aspiration, Imani used it as motivation to flex her resiliency muscle and strived to set realistic expectations for herself and make room for the occasional less-than-ideal parenting moments. The irony for Talia (and for all of us who get caught up in chasing perfection) was that the harder she tried, the more she seemed to fall short. The stronger her fear of failing, the more "failures" she experienced. Talia was stuck in a revolving door of constant parenting anxiety and guilt, with frustration, shame, and procrastination blocking her exit to a calmer, more satisfied life.

Can you relate to Talia's struggle to accept imperfect living when she's determined to achieve perfection? Have you experienced how this can lead to a life filled with too much stress and anxiety and too little joy and pleasure?

This chapter will help you learn to:

- Identify unrealistic parenting expectations and how they keep you far from the parent you want to be

- Embrace imperfect parenting with compassion and an openness to growing and learning as you go

- Shift from parent guilt to resilience by aiming for good enough, imperfect living

- Take meaningful action rather than avoid and procrastinate

Parent Guilt

Most parents will sometimes feel guilt and concern about underperforming; these are a very normal part of parenting. A 2015 Pew Research Center survey found that 80 percent of working mothers feel stressed about getting everything done, 79 percent feel as if they are falling behind, and over 50 percent worry about missing important moments in their family's everyday lives. Less than 50 percent of fathers rate themselves as doing a "great" or "excellent" job as a parent, which means over half of fathers worry that their parenting abilities are less than ideal.

It is natural to feel some guilt about not meeting all of the expectations you set for yourself. But when thoughts of what you should be doing better consume you and impair your ability to fully participate in your life, all that self-judgment and regret shift from common and natural to seriously problematic.

Perfectionism: Cycle of Shame and Despair

Perfectionism entails a continuous cycle of striving to avoid making mistakes, to escape punishing feelings of guilt and shame experienced when you get something wrong. But the more you run from these uncomfortable feelings, the more your brain comes to believe that all thoughts and feelings associated with failure are dangerous and cannot be tolerated or survived. From there, your brain will push you even harder to avoid making a mistake. With each perfectionistic thought and behavior, you strengthen your brain's belief that the survival of you and your loved ones depends on your performing all aspects of life flawlessly. And round and round you go, desperately trying to avoid failure and perpetually feeling as though you are failing. The harder you try to be the perfect parent (or the perfect anything), the more flawed you will feel.

Perfectionistic Thinking Traps

It is part of your parent brain's job to infiltrate you with alarming thoughts, highlighting potential mistakes you may make and the associated dangers. Imagine you are in a forest and you pick up a skinny brown object and think it is wood to be used to make a fire, but instead it is a venomous snake. This would be quite a regrettable lapse in judgment. In this moment, it is helpful for your brain to advise *Be careful...make the right choice!* Although your brain continues to send these warning signals, most modern parenting moments aren't quite so life-threatening. You can rewire your parent brain to learn to better distinguish between *big* problems and little life blips by noting when you are stuck in a thinking trap and are mistaking a minor threat for a life-threatening one.

Your anxious parent brain can easily get caught in these five common thinking traps:

1. Extremes: Dichotomous thoughts—always or never, good or bad, right or wrong, all or nothing, with no middle ground

2. Shoulds, musts, have-tos: Thoughts that push inflexible expectations onto yourself or others

3. Social comparisons: Thoughts about needing to be as good as or better than other people in similar roles to avoid judgment (from yourself or others)

4. Inflated responsibility: Thoughts that assume you are responsible for preventing all possible harm

5. Intolerance of uncertainty: Thoughts that signal intense discomfort with not knowing certain aspects of a situation, or needing to know or be as certain as possible

With these five thinking trap categories in mind, try to identify them in the following thoughts from Talia's parent brain:

a. *I need to make sure that other people think my child is a good kid.*

b. *I keep trying, but I always mess something up.*

c. *What if my mistakes cost my child their future success?*

d. *I have to do everything the right way.*

e. *All these parents are having fun with their kids; why can't I do the same?*

What other thoughts keep you trapped in the perfectionism cycle? See if you can come up with one or two thoughts for each parent thinking trap.

(Answers: a=3, b=5, c=4, d=2, e=3)

When in Doubt, Avoid

When your amygdala signals your parent brain that any and all mistakes will have catastrophic consequences, it is reasonable for your brain to determine that the best course of action is to not take any chances and avoid the potential for mistakes at all costs. Consequently, the urge to procrastinate and avoid engaging in tasks where there is a chance you will make a mistake is a natural by-product of chasing perfectionism. If you allow yourself zero room for error, and the experience of underperforming is so aversive for you, of course you will want to procrastinate and avoid the exhausting effort it requires to always do an A+ job.

Before you know it, you have put off your to-do list and are sitting on the couch engaging in mindless scrolling, which then intensifies your anxiety and guilt. You notice that this might lessen your anxiety in the moment (*Hey, at least I did* something!) but increases your distress later when you realize all you've left undone. And now you are stuck in that revolving door of anxiety, guilt, avoidance, frustration, and shame.

Your Parent Brain Striving for Perfection

There is much research to back up the negative consequences of perfectionism. It is linked to exhaustion and burnout, which then affects physical and mental health (Hill & Curran, 2015; Molnar et al., 2006). Higher levels of perfectionism take a toll on the parenting experience and can lead to feelings of burden and low satisfaction (Piotrowski, 2020). And parents who procrastinate or avoid often are more likely to feel low energy, have low self-confidence, and experience other symptoms of depression (Ferrari & Tice, 2000).

Avoidance and procrastination of important tasks are common responses for parents feeling the pressure to perform perfectly. Under such pressure, it is natural to put off completion of a task or avoid it altogether in an effort to escape discomfort. Unfortunately, avoidance of anything you can't complete perfectly is not good for your brain. Research has shown that the amygdalae in self-identified procrastinators tend to be larger than those who engage in less avoidance. With a larger amygdala, the threat of an action's negative consequences looms large, sapping the person's motivation. Procrastinators have weaker neural connections to other vital areas of the brain, including the dorsal anterior cingulate cortex (DACC), an area of the PFC that helps the body filter out distracting emotions and take action (Schlüter et al., 2018).

Feelings of guilt and shame are also associated with the brain in avoidance mode. When your life's inevitable imperfections leave you feeling flawed and unworthy, your amygdala interprets this as a sign that the challenges in your life are dangerous and must be avoided. From there, it becomes all the more difficult to address the issue at hand because your amygdala has flagged it as an active threat. And round and round the perfectionism-avoidance cycle goes, as we anxiously procrastinate rather than proceeding with a "good enough" solution.

> *Talia, like many parents, knows the perfectionism-avoidance cycle well. She still remembers the tight grip anxiety had on her when it came time for her son's sixth birthday party. Talia had been thinking about this for months, as she and her son attended other kindergarteners' birthday parties. She felt the stress building as she tried to mingle with other parents. Each party seemed even more picture-perfect than the last, with coordinated decorations, plentiful treats, and happy kindergarteners and parents, all perfectly entertained. I'll never be able to pull together something like this, she thought to herself. Too overwhelmed to begin to plan a perfect party, Talia put it off and avoided thinking about her son's festivities until his birthday was a week away. Frantic and embarrassed with her last-minute planning, Talia settled for a low-key birthday with immediate family only. While she knew her six-year-old was happy on his birthday, no matter what, she couldn't help but feel guilty and ashamed that she had backed down from hosting a special party out of fear of failure.*

Imperfect Living for Two

The pressure to be a perfect parent is real. And as you know, it is difficult to let go of the illusion of perfection and stop chasing this unattainable goal. Just remember that letting go of perfection does much more than just alleviate your own stress and anxiety—it has significant benefits for your whole family.

Research shows that children living in an environment infused with unrealistically high expectations can actually come to believe they are not good enough and experience higher rates of anxiety and depression (Hong et al., 2017; Soenens et al., 2008). In many parents' efforts to provide their child with well-intentioned support and high expectations, they end up negatively influencing their child's mood, self-confidence, and overall sense of self. Just as adults feel stress and anxiety when chasing perfection, so do children. Perfectionistic parenting also models an intolerance of failure and reinforces avoidance of taking chances and engaging in activities outside of a child's comfort zone. When parents avoid taking chances and enjoying whatever comes of it, children avoid risks and unknowns, losing out on the chance to try new things and enjoy all that life has to offer.

When you let go of perfection and embrace imperfect living, you open up yourself and your child to a world of possibilities. When imperfection is expected and embraced, rather than avoided, your family is free to try new things, take on challenges and new life experiences, and make memories together, no matter the outcome.

Time to Practice Imperfect Living

Now that we have made the case that perfect parenting is an illusion (at best) and, in its worst form, a trap that keeps you locked out of joyful living, let's get to the hard, important work of rewiring your parent brain to tolerate and find pleasure in perfectly imperfect living, in three steps:

1. Make the choice to tolerate the short-term emotional discomfort of moments of imperfect parenting in order to realize the long-term benefits of a more attuned, connected relationship with your child.

2. Assess the aspects of life where the perfect parenting trap is holding you hostage and define specific behavioral goals to begin working your imperfect parenting mental circuitry.

3. Take daily action to practice engaging in "good enough" yet engaged parenting.

Pause and reflect on these three steps. Check in with yourself and note any initial discomfort that may have come up after reading them. Feeling any resistance to allowing yourself to give up your quest for perfection? This is normal and expected. Lean into whatever feelings come up for you and read on.

Parent Brain Rewiring Exercise: Imperfect Parent Mantras

It might feel terrifying to even entertain the idea of being an imperfect parent. Good! That's how you know you are working on something important to you and worthy of the hard work ahead. To help guide you through any discomfort, practice using a few of these statements:

- I embrace the freedom that comes with imperfect living.

- Bring on the discomfort! I know that means I'm getting closer to more effective and meaningful living.

- I am allowed to have realistic expectations for myself and others, even if these feel lower than what I am used to.

- My kids are allowed to think I am far from perfect.

- There's that unhelpful, but temporary, "I Can't Handle Anything" story in my mind.

- I am/Others are allowed to make mistakes.

- I want to feel all the feelings that come with living imperfectly.

- I am striving for B+ versus A+ living.

On a sticky note, write down two or three imperfect parent mantras to practice during the week. Or just write down a keyword or image that will jog your memory without others having to know what it means. Stick these mantras where you'll see them throughout the week.

Talia placed these quick reminders in her wallet, bathroom mirror, daily planner, and dashboard. Each time she saw them, she repeated the phrase in her mind and exposed herself to the initial discomfort, welcoming the very feelings and thoughts she'd tried so hard to escape. With practice, it became easier for her to move through her discomfort during parenting challenges, rather than plunge into the fear-fueled thought spiral that normally would have kept her stuck.

Embrace Failure

To rewire your parent brain for imperfect living, your first step involves your *willingness*.

- Are you *willing* to experience failure, in service of living a valued (and less mentally exhausting) life?

- Are you *willing* to sit with the discomfort or guilt of not getting it all done?

You are probably already experiencing these things. The difference now is that you can open up to these experiences *with intention*. Instead of resisting what is already there, you can get ahead of your anxious parent brain by embracing these feelings of discomfort. Remember, the more you resist, the more they will persist.

When you are willing to experience discomfort, you notify your parent brain that it does not need to sound the danger alarm. And if your brain doesn't need to prepare your body for a true plan of attack, it now has more resources for the important rewiring that will help you move past parenting perfection and toward more effective, authentic living.

Willingness does not ensure any particular outcome. Many parents we work with fear that if they are embracing failure, they are signing themselves up for even more parenting failures and guilt (to which they say "No, thanks!"). If that were true, we'd probably say that ourselves. However, just because you are willing to open up to imperfection doesn't mean you will experience parenting disasters. What you will experience is much less mental struggle. No more using up your energy to fight off unwanted thoughts and feelings, or exhausting yourself by doing everything possible to avoid them. Now you can use your precious energy where it really counts—for you and your loved ones.

Parent Brain Rewiring Exercise: Chasing Imperfection

Over the next week, ease into imperfection by engaging in parenting "failures" on purpose. Guilt might show up when you make a parenting mistake, but it doesn't have to take up all your headspace. You are allowing yourself to make mistakes with intention so that your anxious parent brain can put that distress tolerance into practice! Approach this with a sense of lighthearted playfulness and curiosity. Who knows—when you let yourself be imperfect, you might even have fun.

Our clients shared these intentional parent failure exposures:

- Repeat "I am a bad parent" fifty times.

- Leave out needed utensils when packing your child's lunch.

- Call your child by their sibling's name five times (at different times).

- Don't leave detailed instructions for a babysitter or caregiver.

- Let your child stay up an hour later than usual.

- Mess up a family meal by leaving out an important ingredient.

- Send your child to school in clothes that don't match.

- Forget to pick up your child's favorite snack from the store.

- Leave dirty dishes in the sink.

- Complete only two tasks on your lengthy to-do list.

- Hold a "mistake" competition with your family and see who can make the most silly mistakes in one night.

Pick three exposures you are willing to practice. Remember, your goal is to lean into these "mistakes" without fighting off feelings of guilt and failure. If you notice any resistance coming from your anxious parent brain, lean on your imperfect parent mantras for assistance.

In your Training Journal, create a chart to track your progress with each exposure. In the chart, create four rows to track your experience at different times: before the "fail," ten minutes after, the next morning, and two days later.

For each time tracked, give these two ratings:

1. Your level of discomfort, from 0 = low (*I'm feeling slightly uncomfortable*) to 10 = high (*worst feeling I've ever had—panic!*)

2. Your level of willingness, from 0 = low (*I can't be okay with this; what the heck am I doing?!*) to 10 = high (*Yup, here I go—I am open to feeling like a parenting failure*)

At the end of the week, what has happened to your level of distress? Does it matter as much as it did at the start of the week? What patterns did you notice with your discomfort and willingness ratings? Write down any insights you discovered.

Bonus points: Create your own parenting fail exposure! The key is to bring on discomfort with intention. Notice any thoughts that involve shoulds or worries about judgments from others—that is usually a great place to start! Do the opposite of what your anxious parent brain is demanding from you.

Redefine Imperfect Parenting

When your child makes a mistake, do you believe they are a bad kid? Even if in the parenting chaos this thought flashes in your mind, do you believe it for longer than a few minutes? A few seconds?

How often do you label yourself a bad parent when you make a mistake? The more you do this, the louder your parent brain hears that it should associate imperfection with *bad*. You can move away from the all-or-nothing thinking and refocus on your learning opportunities. When it comes to parenting, a good/bad label is a hasty, inaccurate, and super unhelpful way of thinking. It focuses on the outcome, not the effort you put forth. Are there other, external, out-of-your-control factors that can influence an outcome? Yup! Are there any external factors influencing your effort? No! You are in control of how much effort you make.

A more helpful perspective might be that mistakes mean:

1. You are human.

2. You might need to try again.

3. You might need to try again, differently.

Do you sigh with frustration that you'll never get this parenting thing right, or could you see mistakes as opportunities to grow? Adopting a *growth mindset* is key. This term, coined by Stanford professor Carol Dweck, emphasizes the importance of effort and learning. A growth mindset believes that abilities and skill sets can be developed, whereas a fixed mindset suggests that these are innate and unchangeable (Dweck, 2006). Luckily for you, when it comes to parenting, opportunities to flex your growth mindset muscle are endless! Any time your thoughts shift to any of the thinking traps outlined earlier in the chapter is a golden opportunity to shift your expectations. You are helping yourself think more realistically and modeling to your child that mistakes are an expected and helpful part of the learning process.

Parent Brain Rewiring Exercise: Bring on the Mistakes

In your Training Journal, make a list of all the parenting mistakes you made during the past week. Beside each mistake, reflect and take note:

1. How did I respond to my mistake?

2. Can I keep learning by either trying something different or accepting that I'm a busy human who makes mistakes?

3. Why is it important for me to keep growing as a parent?

This exercise helps you learn even more about your parenting values, which can serve as a springboard toward your newfound mistake-appreciating parenting approach.

Shift Your Expectations

Unrealistic, rigid expectations for yourself (or others) inhibit your ability to learn and grow. You become stuck in a metaphorical hamster wheel of perfection, trying to outrun failure, and failing. With realistic expectations, you open yourself to the possibility of stopping, and you can now more clearly see how to step out of the hamster wheel. You can continue to model a growth mindset to your child by voicing your thoughts aloud, as if narrating your thought process. This helps your child begin to organize their own thoughts and think flexibly.

Parent Brain Rewiring Exercise: Find Your Own Imperfect Parenting Style

1. In your Training Journal, list at least ten of your parenting expectations. Write anything that comes to mind. You could start your list by completing these sentences:

   - A parent should…

   - As a parent, I have to…

   - I need to make sure that…

2. Beside each expectation, estimate the effort required (low, medium, high).

3. Label each one "realistic" or "unrealistic." A realistic expectation is one that is *specific* and *attainable* with low to medium effort (not by running yourself into the ground!).

For any unrealistic parenting expectations:

- Say them out loud as you picture a critical boss making unreasonable demands, or an annoying salesperson who is lying to convince you to buy.

- Practice infusing flexibility into this expectation. How can you make it into more of a realistic goal? Hint: Try replacing a "should" with "would like to."

Here's how Talia completed this exercise:

I should always help with homework, even after a long day at work.

   - Effort: High

- Expectation: Unrealistic

- Realistic Expectation: I would like to help with homework when I can, so after a long day at work I can spend a few minutes reviewing if they have any questions or ask my partner to step in for homework duty.

Take Action to Do Less

Do *less?!* You might be perplexed by this guidance. Isn't procrastination the issue? There are two possible situations here:

1. You are doing too much of the unimportant things in order to avoid the actually important (but anxiety-inducing) tasks. For instance:

   - Completing all the easy, stress-free tasks first

   - Overorganizing your calendar, to-do lists, or other low-priority tasks

2. You are not doing enough because you are too overwhelmed by your own or others' expectations, and it's too hard to even try. Examples include:

   - Telling yourself it will take much longer to do a simple task than it actually will, so you put it off

   - Planning to prepare or research information so you can completely complete a task, leaving no room for errors or critiques from others, which feels impossible, so you don't even start

We want you to take action where it counts. Have you heard of the 80/20 rule, or the Pareto principle? It says that 80 percent of the outcome can be attributed to 20 percent of the efforts you make. So why overload yourself with so many expectations when your goal can be reached by doing less? And with a smaller mental to-do list, it will be so much easier to proceed with the important tasks.

Just like muscles, the mental circuitry that helps you push past unhelpful thoughts and feelings to get things done can be strengthened with repetition.

Each time you engage in an avoided task, you help your parent brain build distress tolerance and learn that the task wasn't as terrible as you had predicted. Or, if it was, then your parent brain learns that you are resilient and can handle it. Bonus: You are leading by example—by taking action to do less, you are modeling to your child that they too are resilient enough to take the more effective, albeit uncomfortable, course of action.

Parent Brain Rewiring Exercise: Flex Your "Just Do It" Muscle

Pick a task you have been putting off. It could be a small chore or a yearlong project. Rate how uncomfortable you feel when you think about starting this task, on a scale of 0 to 10.

1. Start with 10 percent. Decide what your first step would be, one that requires only about 10 percent of the total effort required. It might be opening up a document. It could be rolling out your yoga mat. Maybe it is chopping up vegetables for dinner. Or writing ten sentences. You get to choose what 10 percent looks like for you.

2. Activate your "just do it" muscle. Time to take action. Notice thoughts of resistance, and refocus on a countdown from 5. Then refocus on your steps to getting started. It can be helpful to narrate your actions as you go: "Two feet on the floor. Stand up. Sit down at the desk. Open the document. Fingers on the keyboard. Type the first sentence."

3. Check in with yourself. Was that doable? Did it feel as bad as you thought? Note your new rating of discomfort after you complete your 10-percent step.

4. Game plan. Can you keep the momentum going? If yes, repeat the process with your next 10-percent step. If not, refrain from self-judgment and take a break. Use some strategies from earlier in the chapter to move toward imperfection. Can you connect to a value behind this task? After fifteen to twenty minutes, see if you can start with your next 10-percent step on the same task.

How These Perfectly Imperfect Exercises Rewire Your Parent Brain for Less Stress and Anxiety

When you do everything in your power to avoid making mistakes, you imprison yourself in a teeny tiny world of certitude, and what is the fun of that? Life's most joyful and satisfying moments occur when you explore and engage with novelty. And by providing your brain with fewer opportunities to "get it wrong," it doesn't get the rewiring enhancements that come with learning that you can handle and in fact grow from life's unexpected and unplanned-for moments. By teaching your parent brain to tolerate your imperfection, you open yourself up to joy, happiness, and deep connections to the aspects of your life most important to you. When you take a risk, make a mistake, and move forward, you teach your amygdala that you can handle occasional moments of failure and therefore it need not panic the next time you step outside your comfort zone. Your life and your child's life don't depend on always getting everything right. By activating your brain's "just do it" muscle—despite feeling overwhelmed and fearful of underperforming—your parent brain will be one step closer to operating in a perfectly imperfect state, as it learns that even if you "fail" you can handle it and proceed with valued living.

CHAPTER 10

Maintaining Your Gains

You made it! It has not been easy work to read through and engage in all of the suggested exercises in this book. You kept at it, determined to proceed with the important work of rewiring your parent brain to experience less stress and anxiety. You began this journey with us by assessing how your brain operated "on parenting." This final chapter will help you consolidate all your hard work and define an action plan you can continue to engage in. Again, maintaining healthy parent brain functioning is not an end in itself, just as maintaining maximum physical health is not a destination you one day reach. Maintaining both mental and physical fitness takes ongoing commitment you must renew every day. This chapter will help you create an action-oriented, sustainable parent brain wellness plan.

Your Balanced Parenting Scorecard: The After Snapshot

Let's take a snapshot of your progress with a post-training assessment of your current parent brain strengths and challenge zones, just as you did at the outset.

Take a moment to think about this past week. Provide a rating, on a scale of 0 to 10 (with 0 being not at all and 10 being very much so), of the extent to which you agree with each of these statements:

Self-Compassion

1. I strive to be self-compassionate rather than self-critical.

2. I can recognize when I am stuck in self-judgment and not working toward finding a solution to improve my situation.

3. I can notice myself having a self-critical thought without believing that judgment represents truth.

4. I can shift from beating myself up to more effective problem solving.

5. I can compassionately guide myself through stressful situations.

Total Self-Compassion score: _____

Realistic Thinking

1. I can notice when my mind is stuck in negative thinking mode.

2. When I am stuck in a negative thinking loop, I can disengage from these thoughts and bring my attention back to the present moment.

3. When I find myself worrying about my child's well-being, I can evaluate the situation logically, rather than emotionally.

4. I feel equipped to challenge unhelpful worry thoughts so I can stay in the moment with my family.

5. I can distinguish between a true problem to be solved and general life uncertainty to be tolerated.

Total Realistic Thinking score: _____

Mindfulness

1. I can fully engage in the present moment when I spend time with my children.

2. I can listen and actually hear what my child is expressing as we talk.

3. I feel connected to my child as we engage in activities together.

4. Throughout the day, I can notice distracting mental noise and then gently bring my attention back to the current moment.

5. Even during times of high anxiety and stress, I can remain present with my family.

Total Mindfulness score: _____

Freedom from Your Past

1. I can experience reminders of painful moments from my childhood without becoming overwhelmed or avoidant.

2. Difficult moments from my past do not prevent me from living a full life in the present.

3. I can separate the difficult moments I had in my childhood from my fears and concerns for my children.

4. When my child is feeling emotional pain or distress, I can believe in their resilience, rather than feel triggered and overwhelmed by the need to rescue them.

5. I can differentiate between when I am truly in danger and when my brain is experiencing a false alarm.

Total Freedom from Your Past score: _____

Emotional Regulation

1. I can calm myself down and cool off my emotional temperature when I feel stressed, frustrated, or anxious.

2. During stressful parenting moments I can take the time to first calm myself down and then choose how to proceed, rather than letting my emotional reactions call the shots.

3. I am aware of and can predict which parenting situations are most likely to stress me out and cause me to feel out of control.

4. I proactively plan for how I will try to calm myself down in common stressful parenting situations.

5. I am proud of how I model self-regulation for my children, even during life's stressful moments.

Total Emotional Regulation score: _____

Limits of Control

1. I strive to choose my battles with my child carefully, based on our family values and the aspects of life that are nonnegotiable.

2. I can recognize when my attempts at controlling the uncontrollable are backfiring, causing tension in my relationship with my child.

3. I understand and accept that as much as I care about my child and want to protect them from experiencing any harm or suffering, there is only so much I can control about how their life will unfold.

4. I strive to reserve my parenting energy for maximizing meaningful interactions with my child rather than attempting to control my child.

5. I believe in my child's resilience and ability to handle life's obstacles, even if their path forward is not exactly the same path I would have chosen for them.

Total Limits of Control score: _____

Valued Living

1. Making time for myself and my own needs is a priority in my life.

2. I can give time and attention to my children's activities and interests, while also giving time and attention to my own activities and interests.

3. I strive to engage in behaviors and activities that align with my values and priorities.

4. Every day I make the time to reenergize with moments (big or small) of relaxation, enjoyment, or connection with something I truly care about.

5. My child (or other family members) could tell you what my personal values and interests are.

Total Valued Living score: _____

Perfectly Imperfect Parenting

1. I am an imperfect parent, and that is okay with me.

2. When faced with a seemingly impossible parenting to-do, I can take small action steps to address the situation, instead of avoiding due to fear of messing up or being judged.

3. I am allowed to make mistakes.

4. I accept "good enough" living over perfection, which leaves me with more time to be present and enjoy the moment with my family.

5. I know that doing my best (whatever my best may look like on any given day) is good enough for myself, my partner, and my children.

Total Perfectly Imperfect Parenting score: _____

Your Balanced Parenting Scorecard After Snapshot

Balanced Parenting Skill	Total Score (0–50)
Self-Compassion	
Realistic Thinking	
Mindfulness	
Freedom from Your Past	
Emotional Regulation	
Limits of Control	
Valued Living	
Perfectly Imperfect Parenting	

Understanding Your Results

If your total Self-Compassion score is:

0–20: You deserve a whole lot more of this important capability.

21–40: You are doing a good job of offering yourself self-compassion, but you deserve even more of it.

41–50: You are nailing the ability to offer yourself self-compassion instead of getting stuck shaming and blaming yourself about parenting mistakes.

If your total Realistic Thinking score is:

0–20: You deserve a whole lot more of this important capability.

21–40: You are doing a good job of thinking realistically rather than catastrophically, but you deserve even more moments experiencing life from this perspective.

41–50: You are nailing the ability to move through stressful parenting moments with a realistic rather than catastrophic mindset.

If your total Mindfulness score is:

0–20: You deserve a whole lot more of this important capability.

21–40: You are doing a good job of living life in the here and now, but you deserve even more moments experiencing life from this perspective.

41–50: You are nailing the ability to live life mindfully, fully present in the here and now.

If your total Freedom from Your Past score is:

0–20: You deserve a whole lot more of this important capability.

21–40: You are doing a good job of not letting pain and suffering from your past get in the way of living life to the fullest, but you deserve even more moments experiencing life from this perspective.

41–50: You are nailing the ability to move through and past prior times of pain and suffering, allowing you to live your current life to the fullest.

If your total Emotional Regulation score is:

0–20: You deserve a whole lot more of this important capability.

21–40: You are doing a good job of calming yourself down when you are feeling stressed and anxious, but you deserve even more of the ability to regulate your emotional temperature.

41–50: You are nailing the ability to regulate your emotional temperature and model for your child how to transition from feeling out of control and emotionally reactive to a calm and grounded operating mode.

If your total Limits of Control score is:

0–20: You deserve a whole lot more of this important capability.

21–40: You are doing a good job of understanding where the control you have over your child stops and theirs starts, but you deserve even more of the ability to direct your emotional energy toward strengthening your connection and sharing moments of joy with your child.

41–50: You are nailing the ability to choose your battles and know when to try to control your child and when to believe in their resilience and ability to handle aspects of life on their own terms.

If your total Valued Living score is:

0–20: You deserve a whole lot more of this important capability.

21–40: You are doing a good job of differentiating between who you are as a parent and who you are more widely, but you deserve even more moments to engage with the things that energize and revitalize you most.

41–50: You are nailing the ability to fulfill your role as a parent while also maintaining your own values and cultivating the aspects of your life that inspire, energize, and fill you up the most.

If your total Perfectly Imperfect Parenting score is:

0–20: You deserve a whole lot more of this important capability.

21–40: You are doing a good job of accepting that to be human is to make occasional mistakes, but you deserve even more moments of perfectly imperfect living.

41–50: You are nailing the ability to take chances, learn through doing, and model perfectly imperfect living for your child.

Parent Brain Rewiring Exercise: Mapping Your Parent Brain Progress

1. Map out your Balanced Parenting Graphical Scorecard After Snapshot on the same worksheet you used for your Before Snapshot in chapter 1. (The blank scorecard is available to download at www.newharbinger.com/50300.)

2. Mark each total score on the corresponding parenting skill set for your post-assessment results and then connect the dots.

3. Compare and contrast the parent brain skills you have been able to enhance. Are there any parent brain capabilities that have increased? Do these results align with how you have been viewing your progress as well as the mental circuitry that are your greatest challenge zones?

A completed Balanced Parenting Graphical Scorecard will look something like this.

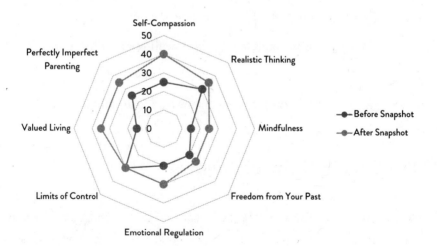

Once you have mapped out your before and after scores, pause to appreciate all that you have done. As you look at your Balanced Parenting Graphical Scorecard, try not to read too much into your scores or place judgment on it.

No matter what, you have been taking solid, worthwhile steps toward becoming a less stressed-out, more effective parent. It will take ongoing dedication and daily practice to continue the work of rewiring your brain to experience less stress and anxiety. You are just taking a pause in your journey, not completing it!

As you compare your assessment results, notice whether any disappointment, self-judgment, or shoulds show up. Maybe some of those thoughts arise; maybe they don't. There will always be work to be done; some balanced parenting skills come easier, others you must work hard to strengthen. Think of your physical fitness; perhaps your legs are naturally strong and toned, but you have to put extra effort and dedication into activating and strengthening your core muscles. There are similar differences in your parent brain's array of skills and capabilities. Rewiring your parent brain to experience less stress and anxiety and more joy is a work in progress, with ongoing fluctuations as you navigate both challenging and meaningful moments. What matters is that you acknowledge your intentional efforts to parent with more joy and fulfillment.

In your Training Journal, take note of the following:

- Did any of your scores surprise you?

- What was your first takeaway from seeing your progress?

- Which parenting skills seem to be parenting strengths for you?

- Which parenting skills present challenges for you?

- Would you like to focus more on any particular skills?

The Winding Road of Progress

Progress is not a steady uphill climb. It is a lengthy journey filled with unexpected obstacles, stressors both big and small, joyous life changes, and continual growth and learning as you adapt to the world around you. The good news is that these skills you've learned will help you better navigate life's ever-changing terrain. As you continue to rewire your parent brain to experience less stress and anxiety and more joy, you will reap plentiful benefits.

By applying the skills you have learned here, you will increasingly be able to move through stressful, anxiety-fueled moments rather than getting stuck in them. You will continue to strengthen your mental circuitry associated with active coping rather than mindless avoidance. You will notice that you have more mental energy to invest in valued living with your family. You will obtain richer, more meaningful connections as a return on this investment of your precious life force. As you experience more moments guided forward by your values rather than your out-of-control emotions, you will experience enhanced joy, peace, and overall life satisfaction.

To Be Human Means Experiencing Occasional Parenting Stress and Anxiety

What is your initial reaction to these words? *Wait, what? I'm going to keep experiencing parenting stress and anxiety?* Does part of you still insist that you can't experience enhanced joy without eliminating uncomfortable thoughts and feelings? Freedom from stress and anxiety does not mean eliminating them. After all, stress and anxiety are critical for survival; without these protective mental states, we would be walking ourselves and our loved ones into all sorts of dangerous scenarios. Freedom from stress and anxiety means learning how to move through and past emotional distress rather than trying to outrun, avoid, or fight your way past life's harder moments.

The goal of all of this hard work you have been engaging in (and will continue to engage in) is to place yourself back in the driver's seat of your life. Stress and anxiety will always be along for the ride, but now you know how to call the shots and decide which path forward you choose to take. When you inevitably notice stress and anxiety attempting to grab the steering wheel to stop your moving in a direction they deem too dangerous for you to handle, you can pause and decide what to do next. You can choose to pull over, you can choose to slow down, you can choose to change direction. There is no wrong parenting move, as long as you act with awareness and intention rather than emotional reactivity.

Nurture Your Parenting Gains

This book has given you the opportunity to upgrade your parent brain to be compatible with modern living. If you remain committed to working out your balanced parenting mental muscles, for just a few moments a day, your brain will keep learning to spend less energy on catastrophic thinking and mistaking false alarms for actual threats, and you'll give more attention to mindfully enjoying shared experiences with your child. To maintain your motivation, treat your brain to frequent reminders of what you have to gain from enhancing and maintaining your mental fitness.

All new learning (and so, new rewiring) is additive. You don't completely remove or delete your historic thoughts, beliefs, or behaviors; you gain new ones. To continue strengthening your balanced parenting mental circuitry, remind yourself: use it or lose it. Brain connections not used over time become weaker and less accessible, to make more space for those more frequently relied on for easier and faster execution.

You've had old thoughts and engaged in old behaviors thousands of times; you have had new thoughts and engaged in new behaviors far fewer times. It can be incredibly easy to revert to your old ways. Kind of like your favorite pair of old, comfy, well-worn (but out of style) shoes—you slip your feet into those, and they fit like Cinderella's slipper. Would a beautiful, well-made, stylish pair of new shoes fit in the same way? Probably not; they'd need some real breaking in. So when you are in the throes of life, feeling stressed with its ups and downs and rushing out the door, which pair of shoes are you more likely to throw on? In the same way, your brain on parenting will readily revert to actions and thoughts you've engaged in most in the past, unless you do the daily work of activating new mental circuitry for balanced parenting skills.

Luckily, our human brains are also hardwired to adapt to new, unfamiliar thoughts and actions. Each time you choose to use one of your new balanced parenting skills, you strengthen the associated neural connections. And as you keep working your balanced parenting mental muscles, it will become more automatic to engage in these healthy thoughts and behaviors in the next stressful parenting situation.

Remember, your brain learns through experience. So even when you start to experience stress-free, low-anxiety days more often, keep practicing. You can use your parenting tools even in carefree moments with your child. And when another stressor appears, you will be well equipped to feel more effective in managing the moment.

The Best Defense Is a Good Offense

The key to maintaining and continuing to build on your progress is to hold an offensive, rather than reactive, posture and always look for ways to work your balanced parenting mental muscles. Through these last exercises, you'll customize your own proactive brain rewiring maintenance plan.

Parent Brain Rewiring Exercise: Playing Offense to Your Parenting Worries

You can get ahead of your anxiety by recognizing key moments when you may be more vulnerable to fall back into old, familiar (stress-fueled) parenting patterns.

Note the following in your Training Journal:

- In which life situations do you usually find yourself feeling stressed?
    - When someone is sick
    - Before a family vacation
    - At the end of the summer, before the school year starts
    - When your kids experience social or academic challenges
    - When your family experiences financial challenges
    - When your job workload increases and you're less available to family
    - When visiting with family or friends out of town
    - When arguing with a spouse, friend, or family member
    - Any others that come to mind
- Are there situations where you can plan ahead?

- How will you know when you're unexpectedly feeling stressed? Where will you feel it in your body? Which familiar worry thoughts or ineffective actions might start to show up?

Becoming aware of key triggers will help you proactively plan for stressful life moments when your parent brain eagerly offers up a flurry of catastrophic worry thoughts.

Parent Brain Rewiring Exercise: Find Your Go-To Tools

In your Training Journal, work through the following steps to identify tools from the chapter exercises that might help you regulate or shift your perspective in anxious moments.

1. **Create a list of the exercises and tools you found to be most helpful.** We recommend writing down the page number each exercise begins on for easy reference.

2. **Next to each exercise or tool, write down the time it takes you to complete it.** Watch out for your brain tricking you into thinking it takes longer or requires more effort than it actually does.

3. **Circle the exercises that you can do on the run.** Since we know that busyness and chaos is a part of the parenting experience, find the tools you can use when you don't have time to sit down and focus.

With this customized, organized toolbox, you can easily access help in tough parenting situations. Whenever you need a refresher, refer back to the original exercises or swap in any similar tools to keep you feeling confident and prepared.

Parent Brain Rewiring Exercise: Planful Practice

In your Training Journal, follow these prompts to plan your daily rewiring practice. The goal is to not get overwhelmed, but to provide yourself with an approachable plan and structure to maintain your personal progress.

- **Set aside time to practice in low-stress moments.** Find ten to fifteen minutes in your week to sit down with your Training Journal and practice a more challenging parenting tool. Take a look at your Balanced Parenting Graphical Scorecard to see which area you want to focus on.

- **Teach your child to use an anxiety-busting tool and practice together.** Three major parenting wins here: you get to practice, your child gets to learn and practice, and you both get to spend quality time together (and even bond over the ups and downs with our friend Anxiety).

- **Set reminder cues to practice.** Do whatever works best for you! Some ideas our parent clients have used are:
  - Writing a keyword on a sticky note and placing it in your car, on the bathroom mirror or work desk, or any other place you may need calming
  - Attaching your practice to a daily action, like brushing your teeth, waiting at a stoplight, or sitting in line at school drop-off
  - Scheduling gentle reminders, either on your calendar app or through a reminder app

- **Schedule a follow-up appointment with yourself.** Set a time three months from now to check in and review your Training Journal. We encourage you to set up a time in your calendar or on your phone as you would with any other appointment. Even if you feel like you don't need to, sit down and see how your Balanced Parenting Graphical Scorecard is looking now. You might find some tools to focus on, or, at the very least, you can applaud yourself for keeping up with your progress

When you take the time to make meaningful changes in your life, you are making a commitment to yourself, your child, and your family. You deserve to take this time to continue rewiring and work toward the life you want. But be flexible with your expectations—you can't (and need not) do it all.

Parent Brain Rewiring Exercise: Note to Self

In your Training Journal, write an encouraging Note to Self. Using self-compassion and realistic thinking, reflect on your hard work. Thank yourself for taking the time to learn new skills and make beneficial changes. Remind yourself that you can keep moving past the anxiety and stress that you know all too well. You have the tools to quiet the noise. Offer yourself meaningful targets to move toward—which values make all this hard work worthwhile?

Here's an example of a parent client's Note to Self:

> I can't believe I actually stuck with this book, even with all the distractions and life events that have unfolded over the past month. Even though there were times I was honestly a bit "over it," I kept practicing. Before, life felt completely overwhelming; now things can still feel intense at times, but it's so much more manageable. It's such a relief, and I'm really proud of myself for dedicating the time and effort to doing this work. I find myself using my go-to tools regularly, and I know I can come back to this book if I'm ever feeling stuck. Note to self: I can do hard things. I'm well-equipped to be a parent and manage parenting challenges, even when the going gets tough. Time spent with my family is so precious, and I want our time together to really count. Seeing the smiles on my little ones' faces makes this all so worth it.

Yours can be longer or shorter—whatever can serve as a quick and helpful reality check to your anxious brain when life gets tough.

When You Deserve More Support

We all need to ask for help at some points in our lives. Your child may receive extra support from tutoring for a challenging subject, or you might connect with your coworkers for accountability in completing a large project. There is no shame in reaching out for support if it helps set yourself up for success.

Seeking help to feel less anxious and stressed is common, especially in this day and age. Many people benefit from therapy. Whatever the reason may be, we know the value in having a compassionate and skilled therapist serve as your guide. We believe that clients show immense strength in recognizing when it's time for that extra support.

While we are confident that these parenting tools will set you on the right track, you may progress more quickly with a trained professional by your side. It can also help you more consistently practice these skills. You might seek therapy if you haven't seen much of a difference between your Before and After Snapshots. You may still feel that your anxiety and stress impact your life daily and frequently get in the way of your family relationships. If you are experiencing significant anxiety and stress levels, you may find it more difficult to fully engage in the brain rewiring exercises, so you may not see a difference right away.

If you find yourself self-medicating by using alcohol or drugs to avoid feeling anxious or stressed, it is important to look for support from a trained professional. In times of severe distress and hopelessness, or if you are experiencing thoughts about harming yourself or others, we encourage you to seek the professional support you deserve.

It might feel overwhelming to reach out for support. You can find helpful resources through organizations such as the Anxiety and Depression Association of America (www.adaa.org). There you can also find a listing of therapists trained to provide treatment for anxiety and related concerns. It might also be helpful to connect with other parents who experience similar challenges and can provide meaningful support or other resources. You can find parenting resources and virtual or in-person parenting support groups through Parents Helping Parents (www.parentshelpingparents.org). They also provide a confidential and anonymous Parent Stress phone line available 24/7 for parents needing support.

Conclusion

You have reached the conclusion of this book, but your journey to becoming a calmer, more grounded parent has just begun. Each day ahead will give you new opportunities to continue rewiring your brain to worry less and enjoy parenting more. There will be times that your parent brain reverts back to shame-and-blame mode. When you feel self-criticism creeping in, realize that beating yourself up will only keep you stuck and that true freedom from stress and anxiety comes with acceptance and self-compassion. And without all that shame and blame taking up your precious mental space, you can more effectively navigate stressful parenting moments.

Every day is a good day to practice disengaging from catastrophic thinking and instead engage mindfully in the present moment. Life is happening here and now, and you deserve to be a part of it. Through your ongoing effort and strength, you can experience the magic of now, rather than getting sucked into your mind's planning ahead or probing the past. By staying right here in the present, you open yourself to fully experience the joy of parenting: to truly hear your child's heartwarming giggle, feel their tight hug after a long day, and appreciate their glowing smile when they beam with pride. The more you work your mindful mental muscles, the more shared experiences of joy and delight you'll have with your child.

You have also been working hard to free yourself from your past, training your brain to better distinguish between your historic pain points and your child's current and future obstacles. But there will always be new triggers and situations where your brain mistakes a threatening moment from the past as unfolding in the current moment. You now know how to guide yourself through these challenging moments. You are strong enough to handle the discomfort; you need not run from it. You can model for your children opening up to uncomfortable thoughts and feelings rather than fighting them. You can continue to strengthen your distress tolerance mental muscles and teach your brain that just because something is difficult doesn't mean it is dangerous. In the process you will continue to rewire both your brain and your child's to operate with increased resiliency.

Also in your balanced parenting toolbox is your new ability to lower your emotional temperature. Each day will offer you a new opportunity to practice calming yourself down when faced with a stressful parenting moment. Each time you activate your emotion regulation mental circuitry, you make it that much easier to calm yourself down the next time. Some moments your balanced parent brain will win; others, your emotionally reactive parent brain will win—but progress is possible in either scenario. When your temper gets the better of you and you act first and think after, you can take a few moments to plan for the next time. There is always an opportunity to learn, grow, and rewire your brain. As always, the more your child witnesses you effectively managing stressful, challenging moments, the more likely they will be to emulate you.

And how about all of that work you have been putting into practicing dropping the rope and relinquishing control over certain aspects of your child's life? Now that you're freed from that nonstop tug-of-war, you have more time and emotional energy to coach and support your child. There will still be times when "because I said so" is the perfectly appropriate response, because that aspect of life is not open for debate. But you can consider the nuances and decide when it is developmentally appropriate for them to take the lead and for you to wait in the wings, there if needed but letting them figure it out on their own. Sometimes they will need you more and sometimes less, but you will continue rewiring your parent brain to respond flexibly rather than rigidly, based on the situation.

It does not matter how many tools and skills you have at your disposal if you are unclear what you are building. Your work to define what you want your life to be about will serve as your current blueprint for getting there. But as you and your child grow and evolve, it is important to revisit this question. You are rewiring your parent brain to experience less stress and anxiety so you will have more emotional energy for valued living. With all your hard work, you're expanding your emotional bandwidth for meaningful living, engaging in effective problem solving, and tolerating uncomfortable feelings—and modeling all of these for your child. Both of you deserve to keep up your practice, choosing to focus your energy and attention on the aspects of life you each find most rewarding.

Living with a more effective parent brain may sound too good to be true. But you have also been working on your ability to tolerate and one day rejoice in imperfect living. You need not get it all right. Some moments are going to be better than others. Sometimes you will thrive; other times you will barely survive—there is room for all of it. By working your "good enough living" mental muscles, you'll be freed from chasing the illusion of perfection—again, modeling for your child how to work hard, learn from mistakes, and persevere despite obstacles and setbacks.

Experiencing long-term, sustainable emotional well-being requires ongoing hard work and commitment. But you understood from the beginning that making big changes would take more than just reading the words in this book. You have been rewiring your parent brain to operate more effectively through targeted practice and action. And the more you activate your effective coping mental circuitry, the stronger those neurological networks become, and the more automatically they will activate in future stressful scenarios. When stressful parenting moments unfold (as they always will), you are now better prepared and equipped to move through these challenges.

As your parenting journey continues, we hope you will carry with you all that you have learned in this book. We hope you will remember the power of your strength and resilience in times of challenge and will take steps to invest in yourself and your well-being each day—not only as a parent, but also as a human being. It is our great privilege to walk alongside parents like you as we all journey through life's twists and turns together. We are so glad that you decided to pick up this book and invest in yourself and your family. The limitless possibilities of parenting with less stress and anxiety await you. Go forth and maximize moments of true joy and connection with your family.

References

Covert, M. V., Tangney, J. P., Maddux, J. E., & Heleno, N. M. (2003). Shame-proneness, guilt-proneness, and interpersonal problem solving: A social cognitive analysis. *Journal of Social and Clinical Psychology, 22*(1), 1–12. https://doi.org/10.1521/jscp.22.1.1.22765

Dweck, C. S. (2006). *Mindset: The new psychology of success.* Random House.

El Nokali, N. E., Bachman, H. J., & Votruba-Drzal, E. (2010). Parent involvement and children's academic and social development in elementary school. *Child Development, 81*(3), 988–1005. https://doi.org/10.1111/j.1467-8624.2010.01447.x

Fabricant, L. E., Abramowitz, J. S., Dehlin, J. P., & Twohig, M. P. (2013). A comparison of two brief interventions for obsessional thoughts: Exposure and acceptance. *Journal of Cognitive Psychotherapy, 27*(3), 195–209. https://doi.org/10.1891/0889-8391.27.3.195

Fan, X., & Chen, M. (2001). Parental involvement and students' academic achievement: A meta-analysis. *Educational Psychology Review, 13*, 1–22. https://doi.org/10.1023/A:1009048817385

Ferrari, J. R., & Tice, D. M. (2000). Procrastination as a self-handicap for men and women: A task-avoidance strategy in a laboratory setting. *Journal of Research in Personality, 34*(1), 73–83. https://doi.org/10.1006/jrpe.1999.2261

Flett, A. L., Haghbin, M., & Pychyl, T. A. (2016). Procrastination and depression from a cognitive perspective: An exploration of the associations among procrastinatory automatic thoughts, rumination, and mindfulness. *Journal of Rational-Emotive and Cognitive-Behavior Therapy, 34*, 169–186. https://doi.org/10.1007/s10942-016-0235-1

Geller, D. A., & March, J. (2012). Practice parameter for the assessment and treatment of children and adolescents with obsessive-compulsive disorder. *Journal of the American Academy of Child and Adolescent Psychiatry, 51*(1), 98–113. https://doi.org/10.1016/j.jaac.2011.09.019

Glass, J., Simon, R. W., & Andersson, M. A. (2016). Parenthood and happiness: Effects of work-family reconciliation policies in 22 OECD countries. *American Journal of Sociology, 122*(3), 886–929. https://doi.org/10.1086/688892

Gordon, I., Zagoory-Sharon, O., Leckman, J. F., & Feldman, R. (2010). Oxytocin and the development of parenting in humans. *Biological Psychiatry, 68*(4), 377–382. https://doi.org/10.1016/j.biopsych.2010.02.005

Guite, J. W., McCue, R. L., Sherker, J. L., Sherry, D. D., & Rose, J. B. (2011). Relationships among pain, protective parental responses, and disability for adolescents with chronic musculoskeletal pain: The mediating role of pain catastrophizing. *Clinical Journal of Pain, 27*(9), 775–781. https://doi.org/10.1097/AJP.0b013e31821d8fb4

Hill, A., & Curran, T. (2015). Multidimensional perfectionism and burnout. *Personality and Social Psychology Review, 1.* doi: 10.1177/1088868315596286

Hong, R. Y., Lee, S., Chng, R. Y., Zhou, Y., Tsai, F. F., & Tan, S. H. (2017). *Journal of Personality, 85*(3), 409–422. https://doi.org/10.1111/jopy.12249

Koran, L. M., Hanna, G. L., Hollander, E., Nestadt, G., Simpson, H. B., & American Psychiatric Association. (2007). Practice guideline for the treatment of patients with obsessive-compulsive disorder. *American Journal of Psychiatry, 164*(7 Suppl), 5–53.

Liu, G., Zhang, N., Teoh, J. Y., Egan, C., Zeffiro, T. A., Davidson, R. J., & Quevedo, K. (2020, July 23). Self-compassion and dorsolateral prefrontal cortex activity during sad self-face recognition in depressed adolescents. *Psychological Medicine, 1*–10. doi: 10.1017/S0033291720002482. Epub ahead of print. PMID: 32698918; PMCID: PMC8208230

Maguire, E. A., Woollett, K., & Spiers, H. J. (2006). London taxi drivers and bus drivers: A structural MRI and neuropsychological analysis. *Hippocampus, 16*(12), 1091–101. doi: 10.1002/hipo.20233. PMID: 17024677

Michelson, S. E., Lee, J. K., Orsillo, S. M., & Roemer, L. (2011). The role of values-consistent behavior in generalized anxiety disorder. *Depression and Anxiety, 28*(5), 358–366. https://doi.org/10.1002/da.20793

Molnar, D., Reker, D., Culp, N., Sadava, S., & DeCourville, N. (2006). A mediated model of perfectionism, affect, and physical health. *Journal of Research in Personality, 40,* 482–500. doi:10.1016/j.jrp.2005.04.002

Obradović, J., Sulik, M. J., & Shaffer, A. (2021, March 11). Learning to let go: Parental over-engagement predicts poorer self-regulation in kindergartners. *Journal of Family Psychology,* advance online publication. http://dx.doi.org/10.1037/fam0000838

Oh, Y., Chesebrough, C., Erickson, B., Zhang, F., & Kounios, J. (2020). An insight-related neural reward signal. *NeuroImage, 214,* 116757. https://doi.org/10.1016/j.neuroimage.2020.116757

Piallini, G., De Palo, F., & Simonelli, A. (2015). Parental brain: Cerebral areas activated by infant cries and faces. A comparison between different populations of parents and not. *Frontiers in Psychology, 6,* 1625. https://doi.org/10.3389/fpsyg.2015.01625

Piotrowski, K. (2020). Child-oriented and partner-oriented perfectionism explain different aspects of family difficulties. *PloS ONE, 15*(8), e0236870. https://doi.org/10.1371/journal.pone.0236870

Rockliff, H., Gilbert, P., McEwan, K., Lightman, S., & Glover, D. (2008). A pilot exploration of heart rate variability and salivary cortisol responses to compassion-focused imagery. *Clinical Neuropsychiatry: Journal of Treatment Evaluation, 5*(3), 132–139.

Rodrigues, A. C., Loureiro, M. A., & Caramelli, P. (2010). Musical training, neuroplasticity and cognition. *Dementia & Neuropsychologia, 4*(4), 277–286. https://doi.org/10.1590/S1980-57642010DN40400005

Schlüter, C., Fraenz, C., Pinnow, M., Friedrich, P., Güntürkün, O., & Genç, E. (2018). The structural and functional signature of action control. *Psychological Science, 29*(10), 1620–1630. https://doi.org/10.1177/0956797618779380

Siegel, D. J. (2020). *The developing mind: How relationships and the brain interact to shape who we are* (3rd ed.). Guilford Publications.

Soenens, B., Luyckx, K., Vansteenkiste, M., Luyten, P., Duriez, B., & Goossens, L. (2008). Maladaptive perfectionism as an intervening variable between psychological control and adolescent depressive symptoms: A three-wave longitudinal study. *Journal of Family Psychology, 22*(3), 465–474. https://doi.org/10.1037/0893-3200.22.3.465

Squire, S., and Stein, A. (2003). Functional MRI and parental responsiveness: A new avenue into parental psychopathology and early parent-child interactions? *British Journal of Psychiatry, 183*, 481–483. doi: 10.1192/bjp.183.6.481

Tang, Y. Y., Hölzel, B., & Posner, M. (2015). The neuroscience of mindfulness meditation. *Nature Reviews Neuroscience, 16*, 213–225. https://doi.org/10.1038/nrn3916

Taren, A. A., Creswell, J. D., & Gianaros, P. J. (2013). Dispositional mindfulness co-varies with smaller amygdala and caudate volumes in community adults. *PLoS ONE, 8*(5), e64574. https://doi.org/10.1371/journal.pone.0064574

Wang, Y., Fan, L., Zhu, Y., et al. (2019). Neurogenetic mechanisms of self-compassionate mindfulness: The role of oxytocin-receptor genes. *Mindfulness, 10*, 1792–1802. https://doi.org/10.1007/s12671-019-01141-7

Wheeler, M. S., Arnkoff, D. B., & Glass, C. R. (2017). The neuroscience of mindfulness: How mindfulness alters the brain and facilitates emotion regulation. *Mindfulness, 8*, 1471–1487. https://doi.org/10.1007/s12671-017-0742-x

Yap, M. B., Pilkington, P. D., Ryan, S. M., & Jorm, A. F. (2014). Parental factors associated with depression and anxiety in young people: A systematic review and meta-analysis. *Journal of Affective Disorders, 156*, 8–23. https://doi.org/10.1016/j.jad.2013.11.007

Debra Kissen, PhD, is a licensed clinical psychologist, and CEO of Light On Anxiety CBT Treatment Center. Kissen specializes in cognitive behavioral therapy (CBT) for anxiety and related disorders, and is coauthor of *The Panic Workbook for Teens*, *Rewire Your Anxious Brain for Teens*, and *Break Free from Intrusive Thoughts*. Kissen also has a special interest in the principles of mindfulness and their application for anxiety disorders, and has presented her research on CBT and mindfulness-based treatments for anxiety and related disorders at regional and national conferences.

Kissen is cochair of the Anxiety and Depression Association of America (ADAA) Public Education Committee, and was recipient of the 2020 Gratitude for Giving Spirit Award and the 2018 ADAA Member of Distinction Award. Kissen often serves as a media psychologist, and strives to further the dissemination of empirically supported treatment information by offering simple-to-understand, practical tips and solutions to help mental health consumers move past stress and anxiety.

Micah Ioffe, PhD, is a licensed clinical psychologist who specializes in the treatment of anxiety disorders across the life span, with a particular interest and specialized training in the treatment of selective mutism, obsessive-compulsive disorder (OCD), and body-focused repetitive behaviors (BFRBs). Ioffe is a member of the ADAA, the International OCD Foundation (IOCDF), and the Selective Mutism Association. She is coauthor of *Rewire Your Anxious Brains for Teens* and *Break Free from Intrusive Thoughts*.

Ioffe utilizes empirically supported approaches in her work with clients, including CBT, exposure and response prevention (ERP), and acceptance and commitment therapy (ACT). Ioffe has authored multiple research publications, and presented her research on parent-adolescent communication and its influences on anxiety and related disorders at regional and national conferences.

Hannah Romain, LCSW, is a therapist and clinical supervisor in Chicago, IL; specializing in the treatment of anxiety and related disorders across the life span. She is a graduate of the University of Michigan, and a member of the ADAA and the National Association of Social Workers (NASW).

Romain specializes in the use of evidence-based practices, including CBT and ERP, for the treatment of anxiety and related disorders—including OCD, panic, specific phobias, and BFRBs. In her practice, she works to harness clients' innate abilities with empirically supported treatments to promote empowered and authentic living.

Foreword writer **Karen L. Cassiday, PhD,** is owner and clinical director of the Anxiety Treatment Center of Greater Chicago, the upper Midwest's longest-running exposure-based treatment center for anxiety disorders. She has served as president of the Anxiety and Depression Association of America (ADAA), and is clinical assistant professor in the department of clinical psychology at Rosalind Franklin University of Medicine and Sciences.

Real change *is* possible

For more than forty-five years, New Harbinger has published proven-effective self-help books and pioneering workbooks to help readers of all ages and backgrounds improve mental health and well-being, and achieve lasting personal growth. In addition, our spirituality books offer profound guidance for deepening awareness and cultivating healing, self-discovery, and fulfillment.

Founded by psychologist Matthew McKay and Patrick Fanning, New Harbinger is proud to be an independent, employee-owned company. Our books reflect our core values of integrity, innovation, commitment, sustainability, compassion, and trust. Written by leaders in the field and recommended by therapists worldwide, New Harbinger books are practical, accessible, and provide real tools for real change.

 **newharbinger**publications